LF

D0153255

Disraeli the Novelist

Disraeli the Novelist

THOM BRAUN

London
GEORGE ALLEN & UNWIN
Boston   Sydney

ALBRIGHT COLLEGE LIBRARY

First published in 1981

This book is copyright under the Berne Convention. All rights
are reserved. Apart from any fair dealing for the purpose of
private study, research, criticism or review, as permitted under
the Copyright Act, 1956, no part of this publication may be
reproduced, stored in a retrieval system, or transmitted, in any
form or by any means, electronic, electrical, chemical,
mechanical, optical, photocopying, recording or otherwise,
without the prior permission of the copyright owner. Enquiries
should be sent to the publishers at the undermentioned address:

GEORGE ALLEN & UNWIN LTD
40 Museum Street, London WC1A 1LU

© George Allen & Unwin (Publishers) Ltd, 1981

British Library Cataloguing in Publication Data

Braun, Thom
    Disraeli the novelist.
    1. Disraeli, Benjamin, *Earl of Beaconsfield* –
    Criticism and interpretation
    I. Title
    823′.8   PR4087

ISBN 0-04-809017-4

Set in 10 on 11 point Times by Red Lion Setters, London
and printed in Great Britain
by Biddles Ltd. Guildford, Surrey.

823.8
B825d

181835

Contents

Preface

Disraeli will always be remembered as a politician rather than as a novelist. That is as it should be. This book, while keeping that political career firmly in mind, is an attempt to approach a better understanding of Disraeli the man through his life as a novelist. It is a book about a career which was dependent, in several senses, on a fictional view of life, and which exhibits all the anecdotal liveliness and psychological interest which we always associate with Disraeli's role as a statesman.

I have therefore structured the book as the story of a life, although the scope of past studies (notably those eminent biographies by Monypenny and Buckle and, more recently, Robert Blake) has meant that I have not felt the need to give more than an outline of those events which did not directly affect Disraeli's career as a novelist. By concentrating on his development as a writer of fiction I have necessarily spent more time discussing his early life than I have on those years when he was a leading politician.

As I have suggested, the book is about Disraeli as a novelist, rather than about his novels. Many of those works are out of print and have been for some time, and it has not been my aim to write a purely literary study of novels which are not easily available and which, in any case, are seldom read. My emphasis is rather on Disraeli's career as a novelist; how it began, what shape it took and how it relates to his political career. While I have, of course, discussed all his novels in one way or another, I have tried to deal with limited aspects of them which, I hope, reflect on his life at those particular stages. My aim has been to write a book which will be readable and of interest both to Disraeli scholars and also to people who have read only one or two of his novels. I have tried, however, not to indulge in the kind of plot summaries which often feature in studies about little-known books. Literary criticism is certainly an important part of my argument but, with one exception, I have tried to balance such passages with biographical matter. The one exception is Chapter 6 which is a literary discussion of the panorama and personages in *Sybil*. Such a chapter, while, I hope, adding to our appreciation of the way the author saw his world, seems justifiable within the terms of this book because *Sybil* is, at the present time, available as a paperback, and is probably the most widely known of Disraeli's novels.

A book of this kind, which tries to balance Disraeli's life against his novels, is bound to discriminate. Certain of his writings are included in my survey because, although not novels, I feel that they contribute to an understanding of his fictional process: his early mining pamphlets, the *Vindication*, *The Revolutionary Epick* and *Lord George Bentinck*.

Other recognised writings by him are excluded because I feel that they do not contribute much to such an understanding: *The Tragedy of Count Alarcos*, *Ixion in Heaven* and the *Rise of Iskander*.

With a few exceptions Disraeli's novels are more important for what they tell us about their author than they are as works of art in their own right. 'Fiction' and 'fictionalising' formed an important part of his life, and this book is an attempt to explore that side of his nature.

THOM BRAUN
October 1980

Acknowledgements

I am grateful to the National Trust and the Bodleian Library for allowing me to quote from the Disraeli Papers. For help given during the research, writing and checking of this book, I would like to thank John Sutherland, Andrew Sanders and my wife, Jill.

to
Mum and Dad

Books are fatal; they are the curse of the human race. Nine-tenths of existing books are nonsense, and the clever books are the refutation of that nonsense.

Lothair, ch. XXIX.

1

Dance on a Tight-Rope

On the morning of Monday 2 May 1870 the main stories in *The Times* concerned British subjects killed by brigands in Greece and the arrest by French police of the man who had intended to assassinate the Emperor Napoleon III. One other report took up a large amount of space. It was a review of a new book and it covered six columns. 'In its essence it is a novel of the day or of the future.' 'The grave and gay, scenes and subjects social and political, men of every character and opinion of every shade, blend themselves so happily that the interest has no time to flag, and you are hurried along in spite of yourself.' 'There is just enough of the trivial and conventional to preserve an air of *vraisemblance*, and the mind finds opportunities of repose, although it is never suffered to sink into torpor.' As the *Saturday Review* of 9 April 1870 had said, 'Mr. Disraeli has provided a new sensation for a jaded public. The English mind was startled when a retired novelist became Prime Minister. It has been not less surprised at the announcement that a retired Prime Minister is about again to become a novelist.'

It was certainly true that the public was surprised. Disraeli had maintained absolute secrecy concerning the project. 'I make a rule never to breathe a word on such matters to anyone', he said in 1872. 'My private secretary, Mr. Montagu Corry, who possesses my entire confidence in political matters, who opens all my letters, and enters my cabinet and deals, as he likes, with all my papers in my absence, never knew anything about *Lothair* until he read the advertisement in the journals.' The reviewer in the *Saturday Review*, writing shortly after that advertisement appeared, summed up the general feeling then prevalent:

> If Mr. Disraeli had announced that, on Monday the 2nd of May, he would sing at the Opera, dance on a tight-rope at the Crystal Palace, or preach a sermon at Mr. Spurgeon's Tabernacle, popular surprise and curiosity would not be more strongly roused than they have been by the advertisement that on that day will be published 'Lothair' By the Right Hon. B. Disraeli, MP. 3 vols. post 8 vo.

Why was it that public sensibilities were so taken aback by the venture of a man whom everyone acknowledged to be extremely idiosyncratic in nearly everything he did? It was quite true that he had written no novel since *Tancred* (1847), the last part of the Young England trilogy, and no book of any kind since the publication of *Lord George Bentinck* in 1851. In fact, Disraeli's writing activities had declined on almost every front, and more than twelve years had elapsed since he had contributed actively as a journalist, when his last piece appeared in the *Press* in February 1856. The bulk of that time Disraeli had spent as a politician in opposition and, considering his literary interests, it is perhaps surprising that his pen had not strayed across the paper sooner and more often. If, however, the insecure nature of the government in the House of Commons was his excuse for literary inactivity during the greater part of that time, certainly after December 1868 and the resounding Liberal victory at the polls, Disraeli found himself with more time than usual on his hands. Gladstone, it seemed, would be safely ensconced in power for some years to come. Now was the time, if ever, to write a novel.

In retrospect such a sequence of events looks obvious enough, yet a large proportion of public voices still affirmed their shock when they realised that their ex-leader was again taking up his pen as a novelist. This was mainly due to two factors – the great secrecy in which the novel was conceived and written, and the fact that it was so painful for commentators at large to accept what appeared to them to be the incongruous mixture of a senior statesman and a writer of fiction.

The secrecy under which the project was brought to fruition was certainly something new in the way Disraeli conducted himself as a writer. He was never the sort of author to commit his literary intentions in any detail to journals or letters, and he cannot be said to have purposely sought the kind of acquaintances or literary circles which formed an important part of his father's life. However, the only other books he had written while he was sitting as an MP – the Young England trilogy and *Lord George Bentinck* – has at least sometimes been the subject of letters and conversations with his sister and close friends like Lord John Manners, George Smythe and Lady Londonderry. When Disraeli began work on *Lothair* no friend or relative was given his confidence. The arrangements for publication were made solely between the author and Thomas Longman, the publisher, and the two of them had decided upon almost everything in secrecy by February 1870.

Such mystery meant that even the closest of Disraeli's society friends and political aides, when they first read the advertisement of publication, were reduced to speculating on the work's origin, content and purpose. Richard Monckton Milnes (then Lord Houghton) summed up much of the general feeling when he said: 'There is an immense and most malevolent curiosity about Disraeli's novel. His wisest friends think that it must be a mistake, and his enemies hope that it will be his ruin.'

Many people were simply shocked because they did not expect this of their leading parliamentarians. Not that politics and authorship together were unknown to Victorian readers. Lord John Russell had led a career which was marked by incessant activity – a good deal of which was literary. Between 1824 and 1829 he published *Memoirs of Affairs of Europe*, between 1853 and 1856 *Memoirs of Thomas Moore*, and his *Life and Times of Charles James Fox* appeared in 1859 and 1860 while Russell was Foreign Secretary. Even Gladstone is remembered by literary historians as the author of *Studies on Homer and the Homeric Age* (1858) and *Juventus Mundi* (1869) which dealt with the same subject. Such political figures, however, when they took to writing, nearly always did so within what were considered the respectable and scholarly realms of memoir, classics and history. Fiction was a different matter, and although Dickens, George Eliot and Trollope had given the novel a particularly stolid character of middle-class respectability since the middle of the century, a considerable part of British society still regarded fiction as incompatible with Victorian *gravitas*. It is true that Bulwer Lytton's political career led to a post in the Cabinet, but he was never a politician to compare with Russell, Gladstone, or Disraeli. Even if society respected him as an ex-prime minister, society had always regarded Disraeli the novelist as something of a Lothario.

This type of response found ample space in the countless reviews of *Lothair* which appeared. Only those in *The Times* and the *Pall Mall Gazette* were, on balance, favourable. There were, of course, the odd remarks which refused to follow the general consensus of sober disapproval. The review in *Hearth and Home* on 4 June 1870, which was squashed between an item describing 'How to Make a Scrap-Book' and an article on a 'Proposed Railway across the English Channel', regarded *Lothair* as a purposely political publication aimed at winning the Tories the anti-Catholic vote. Others expressed differing degrees of appreciation. The *Standard* of Monday 2 May claimed that, in reading *Lothair*, we are reminded of *Tancred* 'which for brilliance is a book unsurpassed – a book in which the author writes as Mozart and Mendelssohn must have thought of music'. And then the *Court Journal*, which appeared five days later, declared that 'Mr. Disraeli's book, *Lothair*, is the greatest bit of fun of the day, and the author surely enjoys that fun most himself'.

Such *joie de vivre* was countered by the weighty deliberations of the more sour critics. The *Athenaeum* remarked that the book would have passed unnoticed if it had been by anyone else. *Blackwoods* and the *Quarterly*, both of which had always been strongly anti-Disraelian, roundly condemned it. Abraham Hayward, a celebrated 'focus of literary intercourse', penned the *Quarterly*'s review and lashed unsparingly at Disraeli, calling *Lothair* a 'failure', an 'outrage', 'a sin against good taste and justice', 'a vast mass of verbiage which can seldom be called English' and 'as dull as ditchwater and as flat as flounder.' Such criticism, however, even though it denied the novel's obvious merits, and even though it reflected the sense of dismay held by the more puritanical sections of Victorian society, was unable to stem by invective the enthusiasm which such a novelty was bound to foster. Indeed 'Disraeli the novelist' was the subject of renewed public acclaim even before *Lothair* went on sale. At the Royal Academy Banquet on the last day of April 1870, in responding to the toast of 'Literature', Charles Dickens welcomed the return to the Brotherhood of Literature of such an 'illustrious' brother as Mr Disraeli. Within a few weeks Dickens was dead and an era had ended. The flamboyant success of *Lothair* with the public seemed to herald a new age of fiction: one which commanded even wider dissemination, greater fame and vaster rewards.

The demand for the book was colossal, and it was quickly translated into many European languages. In the United States too the demand was unprecedented. The eminent American publishers Messrs Appleton began negotiating with the Anglo-American Telegraph Company for an arrangement whereby they might telegraph the whole of the novel to New York in forty-eight hours. They were apparently convinced that the ten days' start which the innovation would give them over rival American publishers would amply repay them for the very large fee which it was anticipated the experiment would cost. However, the directors of the Associated Cable Companies decided that as they had at the time only two cables at their disposal (the 1866 cable being under repair), the transmission of the contents of a three-volume novel would probably interfere with regular business. Messrs Appleton therefore had to bide their time and wait for the novel to cross the Atlantic in the more usual manner. They then printed 25,000 copies, and their anticipation of great sales was justified when they sold out in three days. Even in July *Lothair* was selling at a thousand copies a day, and by October 80,000 copies had found their way into American homes.

Unfortunately the world of massacres and conspiracies, politics and wars, did not pause to allow for an universal acclamation of Disraeli's new work, and on 5 August the novel's publisher, Thomas Longman, wrote to the author: 'Bismarck and the war have had their evil influence on "Lothair"!'[1] Indeed, the outbreak of the Franco-Prussian War did cause demand to slacken for a while, but when, in November, a collected edition of Disraeli's novels was published at six shillings a volume, with *Lothair* as the first book, the 'Lothair-mania', as Longman wrote, broke out again 'with all its virulence. Twice we have printed 5,000 copies, and now we have another 5,000 = 15,000 at press.' It was with much pride that Disraeli claimed, somewhat inaccurately, in the general preface which he wrote for the collected edition, that the book had been 'more extensively read both by the people of the United Kingdom and the United States than any work that has appeared for the last half-century'.

Much of the responsibility for organising this vast and rapid distribution of copies and translation rights for *Lothair* lay in the hands of Thomas Longman. Disraeli gave him licence to deal in the property of the novel as if it were his own, and so conscious was the publisher of the trust which had been vested in him that he became very sensitive of any impediment which he felt might influence his business acumen. Consequently he wrote to Disraeli on 25 April 1870: 'I hope it may not diminish your confidence in my publishing power when I confess that I am detained here [96 Eaton Square] by a slight attack of *Gout*! confined to one foot.' As it happens, gout was to be the least of his worries during the period when *Lothair* was his main business concern, for he was very nearly swept off to a premature grave by a far more dramatic affliction. As he wrote to Disraeli on 22 July,

> I have had an adventure and an escape. On Sunday night I was about to take a vapour bath, when by some accident I overturned the spirit lamp and set my bath garment on fire. I fell on the floor, but as soon as I could get up I jumped into a bath that fortunately was ready in the room and threw the well saturated garment in the blazing spirit on the floor. I am burnt a little about one leg and must still be careful for a few days, not more I hope. It was a wonderful escape and I am thankful.

Even after such a reprieve, Longman's main epistolary concern seems to have been to assure his client that his semi-combustion had not impaired his publishing ability: 'All my own business affairs are not impeded and I hope to be able soon to call at Grosvenor Gate [Disraeli's residence].'

If Longman had had any doubts about the circulation of *Lothair* they were certainly put aside by the timely intervention of an ex-regius professor of history at Oxford, one Goldwin Smith of Cornell University in the state of New York. He identified himself with the character of the Oxford professor in *Lothair* who is described as 'of advanced opinions on all subjects, religious, social, and political', 'gifted with a great command of words, which took the form of endless exposition, varied by sarcasm and passages of ornate jargon', and 'like sedentary men of extreme opinion . . . a social parasite.' Goldwin Smith wrote on 25 May 1870:

> In your *Lothair* you introduce an Oxford professor, who is about to

emigrate to America, and you describe him as a social parasite. You well know that if you had ventured openly to accuse me of any social baseness, you would have had to answer for your words; but when, sheltering yourself under the literary form of a work of fiction, you seek to traduce with impunity the social character of a political opponent, your expressions can touch no man's honour; they are the stingless insults of a coward.

Disraeli never answered the letter, but published it instead, and Longman wrote on 9 June that 'The Oxford Professor's letter is doing its work well. So much so that we shall print again as soon as I have your corrections.'

So it was that print followed print, edition followed edition, and the fame of the novel spread. A horse, a song, a ship, a dance, a perfume and a street all took the name Lothair, while Baron Rothschild named his prize-winning filly after Corisande, the novel's heroine. Indeed, the book's appeal went further than Disraeli could ever have originally imagined, and he was to receive letters which showed that *Lothair* was not read solely by the well-to-do. On 3 May 1870, the day after publication, Edward Poulson wrote to Disraeli from the Metropolitan Railway Carriage and Wagon Works in Birmingham:

> As an ardent admirer of your very interesting and I may say instructing novels – for they do not only interest but instruct the minds of their readers, you will perhaps excuse me for so presumptiously [*sic*] addressing this to you, but as I have seen with feelings of great pleasure and deepest interest that another Novel as [*sic*] emanated from your masterly pen, I wish as a member of that class to which it will be a long time in reaching, namely the working Class, and upon their behalf to ask you if you will as soon as possible issue a People's edition, so that we may have the pleasure of reading, according to what appears in the newspapers the best of your novels.
>
> I have sir read your other novels – I prefer Henrietta Temple and Contarini Fleming to the others – but of course I am not competent to give an opinion upon them, for what suits the taste of one will perhaps not anothers, so the others may perhaps be the best although I prefer those named.
>
> Although in politics I am opposed to you, I think everyone must allow that your novels do show up your talents as a writer to perfection. And if this one does Cap the others I am sure that every one will be pleased to compliment you upon your rare talents and all will wonder how you could find time – whilst being brought so forward in the great political questions of this country – to write such a book.

Another letter came from Evelyn Chambers of Seaford in Sussex on 15 November 1873:

> I have just read *Lothair*, and though I am a poor governess whose

opinion is hardly worth the paper on which I write it, yet I cannot deny myself the satisfaction of telling you how much I enjoyed your book . . .

From the beginning to the end there is not one hateful character! no one whom one would be glad to see hanged head downwards.

Needless to say, a novel by an ex-British prime minister which could appeal to the wealthy and workers alike on both sides of the Atlantic was bound to be a resounding financial success. Longman paid Disraeli £1,000 for the original edition of 2,000 copies, and by 1876 *Lothair* had amassed for him more than £6,000, to which must be added about £1,500 in American sales. It was this unprecedented popularity of the one novel which prompted the issue of the collected edition of the author's works. This appeared in the autumn of 1870, and by 1877 Disraeli had received a further £1,000 in royalties from the collection, before Longman finally bought up the copyright for £2,100. Therefore, it is clear that Disraeli earned at least £10,600 between 1870 and 1877 from the sales of his novels – and this figure was all, directly or indirectly, due to *Lothair*.

Financially, then, *Lothair* was a great coup, and this unprecedented success encouraged Disraeli to begin another novel, *Endymion*, for which Longmans offered him £10,000 – the highest single payment for any one novel during the nineteenth century. But what of its other benefits? It was without doubt the literary performance of the year, and it confirmed Disraeli in his role as the most enigmatic public figure of his day. In political terms, however, it seemed to deepen the doubts about the parliamentary future of the author: doubts which had been prevalent at least since the severe electoral defeat of 1868. *Lothair* was certainly not designed to bolster the morale of the ailing Conservative Party whose cause seemed to be steeped just then in profound hopelessness. Yet Disraeli's greatest political triumphs were still in the future – so it cannot be said that the novel dealt a severe blow to the man of affairs.

Yet there is not doubt that the publication of *Lothair* was an event of great importance in our assessment of Disraeli the man and Disraeli the novelist, if not of Disraeli the Prime Minister. Sir Leslie Stephen, in what must have been one of his most off-key critical pronouncements, once said that *Lothair* was a 'practical joke on a large scale, or a prolonged burlesque upon Mr. Disraeli's own youthful performances'.[2] Perhaps this comment had one merit: the fact that it acknowledged the link that *Lothair* had with Disraeli's earlier novels, even if the acknowledgement itself was misplaced. If for no other reason, the appearance of *Lothair* was a unique occasion because it triggered the re-publication of all Disraeli's other novels. It meant that, at a time when his political stock was temporarily low, the public of Great

Britain was invited to pore over the youthful extravagance of *Vivian Grey* and *The Young Duke*, the romances of *Henrietta Temple* and *Venetia*, and the eastern escapades of *Alroy* and *Tancred*. Disraeli's best friends were afraid that a review of all his past fiction could only draw attention to attitudes, stances and modes of expression which would have best been forgotten.

Those friends did not perhaps realise that Disraeli was a novelist before he was a parliamentarian. They did not perhaps realise that it was through his novels that he had first chosen to interpret life in general, and, more important from our point of view, his own life. Or perhaps they realised only too well. 'My books are the history of my life', Disraeli wrote to Lady Bradford some time after the publication of *Lothair*; 'I don't mean a vulgar photograph of incidents, but the psychological development of my character. Self-inspiration may be egotistical, but it is generally true.'

If Disraeli relied on his own ego for inspiration, then he was surely never short of subject matter. And if books were really the key to the history of his life, it cannot be said that he had anything other than a bookish upbringing. His father was one of the most bookish men of his time, and the atmosphere of the Disraeli home must have played an important part in making sure that the young Benjamin's ego expressed itself through literature. But in order to see what that heritage was, it is necessary to go back to the end of the eighteenth century, when a young man named Isaac D'Israeli was first making a name for himself.

Isaac D'Israeli first achieved literary fame as early as 1791 when he was a young man of 25. He was a celebrated writer at a time when Europe was in the ferment of the French Revolution. He was a member of the generation that included Wordsworth and Coleridge, having been born at a time (1766) when it was still possible for him to take his first creative work to Dr Johnson for a critical opinion. Isaac's life, therefore, looked back to the eighteenth century for its formative influences, and spanned fifty years of hectic turbulence in Europe. By the time he died in 1848, Britain was settling into what we now consider the familiar pattern of Victorian orthodoxy, and the Great Exhibition at the Crystal Palace was only three years away.

Biographers normally portray him as a man of sedentary habits who spent most of his time at the British Museum or in his library at home. As far as his son Benjamin was concerned, however, the writer in general could only exist as an energetic expression of the individual's battle to conquer his world. In 1849, when he was a prominent Tory MP, Benjamin addressed himself to the reputation of his father when he wrote a 'Memoir' for an edition of Isaac's works. By that time the son was motivated to some extent by notions of respectability, and his reaction to literary excess was directed against his father's fiction as well as against some of his own early work. Nevertheless, Benjamin did include his father in a dynamic tradition, and the Memoir consciously reflects a vision of literary heroism:

> The traditionary notion that the life of a man of letters is necessarily deficient in incident, appears to have originated in a misconception of the essential nature of human action. The life of every man is full of incidents, but the incidents are so insignificant, because they do not affect his species; and in general the importance of every occurrence is to be measured by the degree with which it is recognised by mankind. Any author may influence the fortunes of the world to as great an extent as a statesman or a warrior; and the deeds and performances by which this influence is created and exercised, may rank in their interest and importance with the decisions of Great Congresses, or the skilful valour of a memorable field. M. de Voltaire was certainly a greater Frenchman than Cardinal Fleury, the Prime Minister in his time. His actions were more important; and it is certainly not too much to maintain that the exploits of Homer, Aristotle, Dante, or my Lord Bacon, were as considerable events as anything that occurred at Actium, Lepanto, or Blenheim. A Book may be as great a thing as a battle, and there are systems of philosophy that have produced as great revolutions as anything that have disturbed even the social and political existence of our centuries.

As with much of his writing, both public and private, there exists in this passage an attempt not only to assert the potency of the writer in general, but also to justify Benjamin Disraeli's own background through his father as part of a heroic process in a historical tradition of philosophical and poetic action. If it is relatively easy to recognise this trait in several of Benjamin's writings, however, it is less easy to decide how much the father's *personal* literary life influenced the son as a novelist.

Isaac was born on 11 May 1766, the son of a devout Jewish stockbroker and a rebellious mother who hated her religion and her social position. Isaac's adventurous nature led him to run away from such a couple, and he was later found lying on a tombstone in Hackney churchyard. Such behaviour was perhaps a portent of literary ability, for the young man soon began to write poetry, most notably a tract 'against commerce which is the corruption of man' – an ominous subject since his father had made his small fortune by his assiduous dedication to trade. Mr D'Israeli senior was, therefore, unsympathetic when the son presented him with the work, so Isaac took the poem to Dr Johnson's residence in Bolt Court. There he was received by Francis Barber, Johnson's negro servant who was then well known in London, and told to call again in a week's time. On that occasion the literary offering was returned to Isaac untouched, with a message saying that Johnson was too ill to read anything. Isaac would probably have taken this as an excuse and gone home depressed with the thought that, far from being ill, the doctor was presumably not interested in reading the outpourings of a mere youth. It would seem, however, that the message did in fact reflect the state of inactivity at Bolt Court, because within a few weeks Johnson was dead.

Between then and maturity Isaac poured out a stream of literary small beer, while at the back of his mind was the notion that his aim was to produce a thoroughly researched History of English Literature. To some extent the first fruits of this tendency for research and compilation came when the 25-year-old Isaac wrote the *Curiosities of Literature*. The book was published anonymously in 1791 by John Murray, to whom the unassuming Isaac had presented the copyright, but the name of the author leaked out and the young D'Israeli suddenly found himself a literary celebrity.

The book was an anthology of pieces of literary and anecdotal history. As a first success it spawned the various other publications of a similar kind which Isaac was to publish in the coming years, while the ever-popular *Curiosities* was added to and expanded as edition followed edition over a period of forty-three years. The final range of topics spanned included 'Cicero's Puns', 'On the Custom of Saluting After Sneezing', 'Milton', 'The Goths and Huns', 'The Chinese Language', 'Alchymy', 'Ben Jonson on Translation' and 'The Introduction of Tea, Coffee, and Chocolate'. Almost at a stroke the *Curiosities* captured the imagination of the bookish, and not so bookish, community.

In more ways than one the success of the book determined Isaac's future life. He became a famed and respected anthologist, a close friend, rather than a financial dependant, of John Murray the publisher, and a habitual seeker after knowledge. As he grew older he kept to the daily routine of reading and scribbling at the British Museum in the morning, visiting the bookshops of Bloomsbury in the afternoon and then continuing his meandering research in his own library. The result was that Isaac proved to be fecund in his production of various writings, several of which enjoyed a steady popularity during his lifetime. Apart from the books of literary anecdotes and miscellanies, he published romances, poems, novels and his two major histories, *An Inquiry into the Character of James I* and *Commentaries on the Life and Reign of Charles I*.

As far as Benjamin Disraeli's literary childhood was concerned, it was not just a case of what his father read and wrote. The society which his father kept was also important, especially Isaac's friendship with John Murray whose social presence and professional position were to play no small part in Benjamin's own first publications. Washington Irving once described Murray's Albermarle Street drawing room during the second decade of the nineteenth century as 'a great resort of first-rate literary characters', and it was there that Isaac met many of the foremost writers of the day, including Scott and Byron. A scrap of paper in Benjamin's handwriting has survived recording his father's recollection of Byron when the two met, seemingly not for the first time, shortly after the publication of the first two cantos of *Childe Harold's Pilgrimage* in 1812:

> I never knew a man with a more modest, gentlemanly, and perfectly unaffected manner. He was now in full fame, and until he left England I often met him. He treated me with so much respect – I had almost said reverence – that I, being a somewhat modest and retiring man, thought at first that he was quizzing me, but I soon found that I did him injustice. The fact is my works being all about the feelings of literary men were exceedingly interesting to him. They contained knowledge which he could get nowhere else. It was all new to him. He told me that he had read my works over and over again. I thought this, of course, a compliment, but some years afterwards found it to be true.

It would appear that Isaac was not deluding himself because Byron's miscellaneous writings contain many references to D'Israeli.

Benjamin recounts in his Memoir the occasion of his father's first meeting with Scott. Apparently Scott saluted Isaac by reciting a poem of six stanzas which D'Israeli had written in his youth. Not unnaturally Isaac expressed his surprise that such a thing should have been remembered by the eminent Sir Walter. 'Ah!' said Scott, 'if the writer of these lines had gone on, he would have been an English poet', and Benjamin adds a footnote saying that Scott must have been sincere about the verse because he included it in the *English Minstrelsy*. The poem in question is *Stanzas addressed to Laura, entreating her not to paint, to powder, or to game, but to retreat into the country*, and it begins

> Ah, LAURA! quit the noisy town
> And FASHION'S persecuting reign:
> Health wanders on the breezy down,
> And Science on the silent plain.

James Ogden, who has made a study of Isaac D'Israeli,[3] believes that the 'Laura' poem represents D'Israeli at his best as a poet.

Benjamin Disraeli was not unaware of the artistic shortcomings of his father; in another part of the Memoir he says:

> My father had fancy, sensibility, and an exquisite taste, but he had not that rare creative power, which the blended and simultaneous influence of the individual organisation and the spirit of the age, reciprocally acting upon each other, can alone, perhaps, perfectly develope; the absence of which, at periods of transition, is so universally recognised and deplored, and yet which always, when it does arrive, captivates us, as it were by surprise.

Isaac, however, despite his obvious lack of greatness as an imaginative writer, still produced an interesting and varied selection of creative works. He wrote two volumes of poetry, the *Defence of Poetry* and *Narrative Poems*, a collection of *Romances*, and three novels; *Vaurien*, *Flim-Flams* and *Despotism*. A few other poems were published separately in periodicals, and there are some unpublished manuscripts in the Disraeli Papers, including a two-act farce, various poems and a novel of fashion. Ogden tells us of these works that *Romances* proved to be popular (there were three English editions and one American), but that of the others only *Flim-Flams* (of which there were two editions) caused much of a stir.

Our interest here, then, in the novels of Isaac D'Israeli is occasioned not so much by their intrinsic merits, as by the fact that they are the creative prose works of a better novelist's father. As far as Isaac's reasons for writing the novels are concerned, there seems little doubt that they were undertaken as a way of conveying, in a popular format, thoughts which might otherwise appear too dogmatic or political. Something of this purpose can be seen in the wording of Isaac's preface to *Miscellanies* which was written in 1796 when he was 30: 'Writings which awaken our sensibility by fiction, must please more generally than books which only instruct our judgement by truths.'

This view is supported by the novels themselves. The first of these was *Vaurien, or Sketches of the Times* which was published in 1797. In the preface to *Vaurien* Isaac says that he has chosen the *form* of a novel rather than the *matter*; that matter was a full-blooded attack on what he called the 'romantic absurdities' of Godwinian philosophy. William Godwin (1756–1836) represented, within the bounds of political philosophy, an extreme form of individualism which was akin to anarchism. Whatever Isaac may have thought of the cult of the individual which came to be associated with his acquaintance Byron, in 1797 his sympathies were shaped by his classical and ordered heritage, and by the social disorder on the Continent, and he was totally uncompromising in his attack on the *political* applications of Godwinian philosophy. The novel's partisan viewpoint meant that it was read by those like-minded souls who feared the consequences of foreign revolution, and for almost this reason alone the reviews it received were mainly favourable.

A few years later Isaac produced what he called a 'new Scribblement'. This work was published by John Murray in 1805, the year after Benjamin's birth, and was called *Flim-Flams! Or the Life and Errors of my Uncle, and the Amours of my Aunt!* The tone of this novel is much lighter than that of *Vaurien*, although the object is once again to satirise contemporary events, philosophies and public figures. It is a strange work, and in some respects it prefigures the excesses of Benjamin's writing in *Vivian Grey*. For example, in the final volume of

Flim-Flams 'My Uncle' marries 'My Aunt', a character based on Caroline Herschel the astronomer, who then gives birth to an ape. Not surprisingly this causes a rift between the couple, after which 'My Aunt' has an affair with a landscape gardener, and 'My Uncle' disappears in a cloud of blue smoke through attempting to prove that brandy is not *eau de vie*. When we consider that at one point in his Memoir Benjamin describes his father as a man whose 'philosophic sweetness of disposition' was one of his notable characteristics, then it is difficult to understand why the father should have made such tasteless jokes about a respectable lady who was in her fifties.

It is even more surprising when we see how Isaac returned to something like the style of *Vaurien* with his last novel *Despotism: Or the Fall of the Jesuits*. This work, described on the title-page as a 'political romance, illustrated by historical anecdotes', was published by John Murray in 1811, and the preface once again makes clear the author's intention:

> An historical introduction to a fictitious Narrative, has been found sometimes necessary to authorise the novelty of its events, its characters, and its feelings; but a story raising only our transient astonishment, may still fail, by its remoteness from our experience, to excite our sympathy; and read like the epigram, for its close, our attention terminates with our curiosity. Should the Fable, however, be found as full of truth, as of wonder, it may claim regard for something more valuable than itself. No history, whether genuine or fictitious, will be studied without instruction, where the dearest interests of humanity are pursued in its conduct, and involved in its catastrophe.

It is tempting to see in this and in *Vaurien* an influence on Benjamin Disraeli, especially in the son's emergence as the author of the Young England trilogy. However, there is not much evidence to support this. It would be difficult to make out a convincing case for a direct influence on the basis of textual comparisons, and even with novels like *Flim-Flams* and *Vivian Grey*, which *are* comparable in some ways, the similarities are not so great nor so exclusive that one would want to base an argument on them. If one were looking for *direct* links between the works of the father and the son, then one would be better rewarded comparing the effects of Isaac D'Israeli's histories of James I and Charles I on the young monarchist Benjamin. The object here of examining briefly the life and work of Isaac is not so as to be able to show precisely what Benjamin gained from his father, but rather to show how he would have grown up in an atmosphere which was not only literary, but also very varied in that literariness: an atmosphere which spanned two centuries of literary thought, method, styles and genres, and an atmosphere also heavily influenced by the personalities of the literary world.

The mixture of the eighteenth and nineteenth centuries is an important factor. Disraeli grew up in a house where the names of Scott and Byron were almost sacrosanct, yet at the same time Isaac himself was not a supporter of the excesses which are associated with the 1790s and 1800s. This was due partly to his own personal character which everyone agrees was gentle, unassuming and basically conservative. It is also true that Isaac's original hero among the poets was Pope, and it should not be forgotten that when the young D'Israeli composed his own first work, the foremost critic of the day was still Dr Johnson. Thus it was that Isaac, whose mind had been primarily fashioned by the expectations of the Augustans, was facing the turbulent years of the turn of the century when his eldest son was born.

Benjamin Disraeli was born a Jew on 21 December 1804 and was baptised a Christian on 31 July 1817. Such a change of religion affected the young man's education and childhood. Indeed, had he remained a Jew, even nominally, then his whole career would have been vastly different. Until the time of his baptism he attended schools at Islington and Blackheath, where he was excused prayers and where he was given special teaching in Hebrew once a week. To return there after his 'conversion' would have put an unnecessary burden on a boy trying to acclimatise himself to a Christian upbringing, and so in the autumn term of 1817 he was sent to a new school at Walthamstow, near Epping Forest.

Not a great deal is known about Disraeli's childhood and education, and there has been a tendency in the past to supplement what knowledge we do have with passages gleaned from his novels. Such methods may seem legitimate to the presenter of 'Disraeli the Novelist', but, on the whole, it is a form of biography which is unsatisfactory and often misleading. Disraeli's natural instinct as a writer was to glamorise, to exaggerate and to romanticise, and there can be little doubt that in the parts of his novels which deal with school-life he presents not a documented account of his own experiences, but rather an interpretation of his memories in such a way that he creates his own mythological past. Everything is seen on a grand heroic scale. One of the boys in Vivian Grey's school, when angry, foams 'like a furious elephant', while in *Contarini Fleming* the hero sees himself at school on a higher plane altogether: 'It seemed that I was the soul of the school. Wherever I went, my name sounded, whatever was done, my opinion was quoted. I was caressed, adored, idolized. In a work, I was popular.' This novel first appeared with the subtitle 'A Psychological Auto-Biography', and therefore introspection is to be expected. Even so, the experience (if it ever existed) has been refined into a statement of heroic qualities. When we remember what Disraeli said to Lady Bradford, about his novels not being 'a vulgar photograph of incidents, but the psychological development of my character', we will appreciate that such passages tell us not so much about the actual events of his life, but rather the way in which the romantic novelist's mind manipulated experience.

The same thing must be remembered when Disraeli's novels are read for indications of his relationship with either of his parents or the household at Bloomsbury. This passage is from *Contarini Fleming* and describes what happens when the young hero's mother sends him to his room as a punishment:

> I was conducted to my room, and the door was locked on the outside. I answered the malignant sound by bolting it in the interior. I remained there two days deaf to all their intreaties, without sustenance, feeding only upon my vengeance. Each fresh visit was an additional triumph. I never answered: I never moved. Demands of apology were exchanged for promises of pardon: promises of pardon were in turn succeeded by offers of reward. I gave no sign. I heard them stealing on tiptoe to the portal, full of horrible alarm, and even doubtful of my life. I scarcely would breathe. At length the door was burst open, and in rushed the half-fainting Baroness, and a posse of servants, with the children clinging to their nurses' gowns. Planted in the most distant corner, I received them with a grim-smile. I was invited away. I refused to move. A man-servant advanced and touched me. I stamped, I gnashed by teeth, I gave a savage growl, and made him recoil with dread. (*Contarini Fleming*, I, ii)

Such passages give little idea of the relationship Disraeli had with his real mother, yet some of the more useful references in the fiction to his education have been ignored by critics who have read only the revised editions of his early works. The choice of the school at Walthamstow, for example, is normally linked to this passage in Chapter ii of *Vivian Grey*, dealing with the hero's prospects:

> Mr. Grey wished Eton, but his lady was one of those women, whom nothing in the world can persuade that a public school is anything else but a place where boys are roasted alive; and so with tears, and taunts, and supplications, the point of private education was conceded.

This may well reflect what did happen in the case of Disraeli, and some biographers, following this up, have pointed to his autobiographical note to Lord Rowton (Montagu Corry), written many years later, which claimed that at Walthamstow 'the whole drama of public school life was acted in a smaller theatre'. R. W. Davis, for example, has said (presumably interpreting these two passages) that Disraeli 'believed that he had been exposed to English public school life in the small'.[4] This is markedly untrue. Disraeli did not believe he had been exposed to public school education at all; he bitterly bemoaned the fact that he had *not* been exposed to it. Following the passage just quoted from *Vivian Grey* is a line which was omitted from later editions: 'As for Vivian himself, he was for Eton, and Winchester, and Harrow, and Westminster, all at once.' If this statement is too dependent on the very thing I have been warning against, that is, the hero's romantic view of his own life, it is at least supported by the authorial voice in what seems one of its more frank moments two chapters later. It is another passage which was omitted from later editions:

> Those, who, in all the fulness of parental love, guard their offspring from the imagined horrors of a public school, forget that, in having recourse to 'an Academy for Young Gentlemen', they are *necessarily* placing their children under the influence of *blackguards*; it is of no use to mince the phrase – such is the case. And is not the contagion of these fellows' low habits and loose principles much more to be feared and shunned, than a system, in which, certainly, greater temptations are offered to an impudent lad; but under whose influence boys usually become gentlemanly in their habits and generous in their sentiments?

The constant allusion in his novels to characters going to Eton and the like is part of the way Disraeli reinterprets history so as to write into his mythological past a public school education which he obviously wished he had had.

As it happens, the school at Essex Hall in Walthamstow turned out to be, if not positively beneficial, at least not damaging for the emerging creative mind of its most illustrious pupil. The school was run by the Rev. Eliezer Cogan, a man who had had the training of most orthodox Dissenters at the end of the eighteenth century, and a man who was probably not a blackguard. This school had been chosen by the D'Israelis in 1817 because, unlike many of the private educational establishments of the time which catered only for the sons of Anglican parents, Cogan's school accepted Catholics, Protestants, Dissenters and Jews. This meant that although Benjamin had a new religion, he would not suffer a regimen of Anglican orthodoxy; in fact, Cogan maintained a form of worship which had no reference to any particular denomination.

The conduct of the schoolmaster was due partly to his liberal upbringing, and partly to his own educational precepts which were often a reflection of his religious beliefs. For example, in 1817, the year that Disraeli went to the school, Cogan published two volumes of *Sermons, Chiefly on Practical Subjects*, and in one particular piece, 'On the Connexion between Theism and Christianity', he tried to make it easy for almost anyone (other than an avowed atheist) to become a Christian:

> Taking the spirit of our Lord's exhortation for my guide, I will

endeavour to shew, that Christianity may be readily admitted by the man who is first seriously convinced of the Being and attributes of God . . . He who is persuaded that there exists a Being who formed, and who sustains the universe, admits one great truth of which Christianity affords a striking confirmation, and has only to consider whether the great Being has interfered in the government of the world, in the manner described in the Christian scriptures.

It would seem reasonable to suppose that such a prevalent belief at the school would have made it easier for the young Disraeli to adapt to Christianity and to develop his own idiosyncratic ideas on religion, although the young man would probably not have been swayed by Cogan's philosophical position. In fact, in many ways he was the type of man who would have been attacked by Disraeli when he was an adult novelist. Cogan was a follower of Joseph Priestly who published in 1768 his *Essay on the Principles of Government* which advocated the view that the happiness of the majority of the people is 'the great standard by which everything relating to [social life] must finally be determined' – the theory which was taken up and developed by Jeremy Bentham. Disraeli was to rebel against the radical, centralising Benthamism with his own brand of romantic Toryism, and even his early novel *Popanilla*, which appeared in 1828, ridiculed the extravagances of the Benthamites. So, at least as far as Cogan's Unitarianism was concerned, Disraeli was to turn violently against the rationalism upon which it was based.

The real benefit that the school gave Disraeli was not in its positive doctrinal stance, but in the fact that it allowed the mind of the idiosyncratic genius a greater freedom of thought and conscience than would have been possible at many of the more institutionalised English schools. Disraeli may have been there only two to three years, but they were impressionable years, and although he may not have absorbed Cogan's liberalism, he certainly benefited from his liberality, in that he was not constrained to mould his morals to suit a tutor of rigid dogma.

In his work *The Literary Character, or the History of Men of Genius*, Isaac D'Israeli wrote: 'Education, however indispensable in a cultivated age, produces nothing on the side of genius. Where education ends, genius often begins.' By the middle of 1820 Benjamin was back in Bloomsbury, back in his father's library, from where he launched himself into a literary career which was to reach its climax exactly fifty years later with the publication of *Lothair*.

Notes: Chapter 1

1   This and other letters quoted in this chapter and in Chapter 8 form part of the Disraeli Papers owned by the National Trust, which are at present housed in the Bodleian Library, Oxford.

2 Quoted by W. F. Monypenny and G. E. Buckle, *The Life of Benjamin Disraeli, Earl of Beaconsfield*, 6 vols (London: John Murray, 1910–20), Vol. V, p. 168.
3 James Ogden, *Isaac D'Israeli* (Oxford: Clarendon Press, 1969).
4 R. W. Davis, *Disraeli* (London: Hutchinson, 1976), p. 7.

2

Sleight-of-Hand Tricks

People who were closely associated with Disraeli's writing projects had a tendency to catch fire. We have seen how the conscientious Thomas Longman was ignited in 1870, and as early as 1828 Mrs Sara Austen, who, in the previous two or three years, had been at least Disraeli's amanuensis and possibly more, became the victim of combustion. As she wrote to Disraeli in April of that year:

> I am rather out of sorts for penmanship, having had the narrowest escape of being burnt to death – I was writing a note for Miss Tyson – to seal which she lighted a candle & put it *under my hair* as for the moment I leaned over the table – Instantly my whole head was in flames, & but for Louisa's [Sara's sister] hands my muslin frills &c would have caught directly – Most providentially a prettily singed head is all the mischief done.[1]

Two years before, in 1826, and with Mrs Austen's great help, Disraeli first set light to the literary world. He had become, if not well respected, at least well known. It was in 1826 that his first novel, *Vivian Grey*, was published: the book which branded the young Disraeli with a notoriety which remained with him for most of his life. Yet, oddly enough, the novel might never have been published in the first place if, in 1826, Mrs Austen had been 'out of sorts for penmanship'. It was her influence which was instrumental in Disraeli's bringing to fruition the first sustained literary expression of his adult years.

When Disraeli left Cogan's school in 1820 he returned to London to continue his studies at home in Bloomsbury. Isaac D'Israeli, writing in *The Literary Character*, had given the example of the poet Gray to support the principle of such an uninstitutionalised education:

> GRAY was asked if he recollected when he first felt the strong predilection to poetry; he replied that, 'he believed it was when he began to read Virgil for his own amusement, and not in school hours as a task ...'. That the education of genius must be its own work, we may appeal to every one of the family.

It is difficult to estimate the scope and thoroughness of Disraeli's education in his father's library; his own reminiscences and fictionalised accounts do not give a very clear indication of any particular academic regimen.[2] What seems to emerge from the evidence available at present is that he had a restless mind which was not content to confine itself to any one discipline for long at a time. The knowledge Disraeli acquired during his education was certainly not as shallow as some of his contemporaries later suggested, but as far as it went it was more often supplemented by imagination and expediency than substantiated by fact and experience. The dazzling and sometimes perverse nature of that imagination lends weight to the argument that his mind was expansive, rather than ordered in a narrow sense.

It would certainly appear from the written evidence of Disraeli's youth that his grasp of the classical languages was no more than adequate for someone who was finally to enter the top ranks of public life – especially as the subject, in retrospect, invites comparison with Gladstone. In assessing the importance then of Disraeli's education on his career, particularly his early years as a writer, we can appreciate that the very lack of dogmatic discipline, both at Cogan's school and in Isaac's library, allowed his imagination or fancy (and here it is not necessary to make a Coleridgean distinction) to expand and indulge itself. Charles Dickens was later to make the point in *Hard Times* on the subject of education that an addiction to 'facts' led to the stultification of the mind. Even a M'Choakumchild with orthography, etymology, syntax, prosody, astronomy, geography and general cosmography at the ends of his ten chilled fingers could not kill Fancy but only maim and distort him. Fancy was to play a large part in Disraeli's literary career and, some might argue, in his political one as well. We can only be grateful that such a Fancy was not maimed and distorted in his early years.

In the general preface to the collected edition of his novels which was published in 1870, Disraeli said that, in writing *Coningsby* and *Sybil*, his two major novels of the 1840s, he had 'recognised imagination in government of nations as a quality not less important than reason'. The same could be said about his view regarding the government of the individual and the conduct of life in general. Disraeli's imagination was one asset which was constantly being drawn upon; however much he wrote for pecuniary gain (and, indeed, this should not be ignored as a stimulus), he was also a compulsive novelist and fictionaliser because of his instinctive need to give expression and a free rein to that imagination. It was a process by which he fictionalised his own life, political life and life in general, by reinterpreting and redirecting experience through his own fancies and fantasies. It was an imagination based on ambition, stoked and provoked by his reading at home.

Such recourse to the manipulation of 'facts' must obviously

influence our attitude regarding Disraeli's failure to go to university. The supposedly autobiographical Vivian Grey, of course, also opts not to go; but again, as with his schooldays, we should be wary of relying too much on direct abstracts from the novels for our assessment of the motives behind the actions and decisions of Disraeli (and, perhaps more important at this stage, those of his parents):

> The time drew nigh for Vivian to leave his home for Oxford – that is, for him to *commence* his long preparation for entering on his career in life. And now this person, who was about to be a *pupil* – this boy, this stripling, who was going to begin his education, – had all the desires of a matured mind – of an experienced man, but without maturity and without experience. He was already a cunning reader of human hearts; and felt conscious that his was a tongue which was born to guide human beings. The idea of Oxford to such an individual was an insult! (*Vivian Grey*, I, viii)

There seems no doubt that, later in life as he sought to rise in political circles, Disraeli felt his lack of a university education to be something of a drawback, in the same way that his having not gone to public school set him apart from the many emerging young parliamentarians of the day. We have seen that, in the case of the school experience, Disraeli attempted to convince himself and others that he *had* undergone something very like a public school education. As far as university life was concerned the initial feeling seems to have been the same, even if Disraeli's expression of it was slightly different. One cannot help feeling that Disraeli was bitter about not going to Oxford – a place surely famed (whether justly or not) as being a society for making the sort of acquaintances useful for an eminent career on the ladder of public life. Consequently, the passage quoted above would appear to be an attempt to exorcise that bitterness by the depreciation of the merits of a university life. Academe compares unfavourably to the life of adventure.

Again, it would seem that the reason for the continuing lack of a formal education was due to Isaac D'Israeli. Despite the remark cited earlier from *The Literary Character* on the subject of genius, Isaac, like several fathers of famous sons, seems to have been less than fully appreciative of Benjamin's talents. An earlier passage in *The Literary Character* may give us a clue to this attitude:

> Let us, however, be just to the parents of a man of genius; they have another association of ideas respecting him than ourselves. We see a great man, they a disobedient child; we track him through his glory, they are wearied by the sullen resistance of one who is obscure and seems useless. The career of genius is rarely that of fortune or happiness; and the father, who himself may not be insensible to glory,

dreads lest his son be found among that obscure multitude, that populace of mean artists, self-deluded yet dis-satisfied, who must expire at the barriers of mediocrity.

Isaac may well have seen in Benjamin a precocious ambition that was insufficiently matched by talent; or he may have seen a fragile talent which might have been crushed by the formalities of Oxford. It is also likely that the elder D'Israeli was so involved in his own work that he was somewhat insensitive to his most gifted son's promise.

Whatever Isaac's views may have been, in November 1821 he paid a premium of 400 guineas and articled Benjamin to a firm of solicitors, Messrs Swain, Stevens, Maples, Pearce and Hunt of Frederick's Place, Old Jewry. The young Disraeli was still only 16 years old at the time and certainly, if Isaac *was* aware of any blossoming artistic ability in his son, such a course of action would seem to be very odd. Law offices are not the obvious places in which to nurture a young creative imagination. It is true that five and a half years later a firm of attorneys in Holborn Court, Gray's Inn, was to employ a 15-year-old office boy with an infinitely profounder literary imagination, who was to become a far better novelist than Disraeli. But it would be wrong to imagine that the legal environment was in any way a stimulus to creative writing other than by opposition, and finally rejection. If Disraeli and Dickens shared any common ground during the 1820s (apart from law offices) it was really only that of having fathers who were at times less than fully aware of their respective sons' great potential. Where Dickens was to draw constantly on his experience in law offices, and at Doctors' Commons, in presenting the metropolitan panorama of his novels, Disraeli was only interested in recreating his own past in his early novels through the idiom of flamboyance and the genre of that part of society which he wished to join. Ironically it was Dickens who was the first of the two to enter the House of Commons, albeit as a parliamentary reporter. Thus it was that while Disraeli was trying to make amends for his less than stylish education and lack of advancement by inveigling himself into polite and political society, Dickens was noting, among other things, the finer nuances of Gladstone's maiden speech in 1833.

It is not difficult to see in Disraeli's own recollections of his time in a solicitor's office yet another instance of his reinterpreting what must have been a mainly drab existence, in terms which, retrospectively, imply a qualification for his later career as novelist and politician:

> My business was to be private secretary of the busiest partner of our friend [Mr Maples]. He dictated to me every day his correspondence which was as extensive as a Minister's, and when the clients arrived I did not leave the room but remained not only to learn my business but to become acquainted with my future clients . . . It gave me great facility with my pen and no inconsiderable knowledge of human nature.[3]

To doubt that Disraeli's role as a private secretary gave him any great pleasure or experience is not to doubt his honesty in recollection; it is simply to re-emphasise the way in which he was always apt to recall things in a manner which was grander than reality. It was not just that he was careless about facts; he was addicted to romance to such an extent that most of his written reminiscences and novels contribute to a personal mythological past. Biographies of Disraeli have shown, for example, how his account of his own ancestry (which appears among his prefatorial remarks to the edition of his father's works of 1849) is wilfully wrong in several respects, and whenever one reads anything by him which has some pretension of being autobiographical, one must always remain aware that 'fiction' was obviously more to him than just the writing of books for artistic prowess or financial gain. It was more a way of recasting 'life' as heroic and ordered.

This recasting is nowhere more apparent than in Disraeli's adaptation of his own venture into 'society'. Vivian Grey finds himself in the presence of great personages because of the social standing of his father who was 'an honoured guest among the powerful and the great'; but it is certain that Disraeli himself was by no means so well enamoured of society in the early 1820s. His father's friends may well have included one or two literary giants but, for the most part, they were men who had no influence outside bookish circles. Of this set it was John Murray whose influence was greatest, both generally and particularly, with regard to the D'Israeli family.

Disraeli attended some of Murray's dinner parties where the conversation, not surprisingly, revolved around literary matters. He recorded some of the talk on the occasion of a meal on 27 November 1822, when the discussion was about Byron. Thomas Moore, who was also present, said of the poet in exile:

> He's very dandified, and yet not an English dandy. When I saw him he was dressed in a curious foreign cap, a frogged great coat, and had a gold chain round his neck and pushed into his waistcoat pocket. I asked him if he wore a glass and took it out, when I found fixed to it a set of trinkets. He had also another gold chain tight round his neck, something like a collar.[4]

Such flamboyance appealed to Disraeli who reproduced the whole conversation, in only a slightly changed way, in *Vivian Grey* (IV, i).

Surrounded by literariness, it was no surprise when Disraeli himself began to write. When exactly that was is something which cannot be answered with any definiteness, although it would seem reasonable to suppose that by the age of 15 he had begun to indulge in the form of creative scribble which afflicts most adolescents of a sensitive bent.

Disraeli's most early extant creative work was written in 1823 when

181835

ALBRIGHT COLLEGE LIBRARY

he was 18. With his friend William Meredith he produced *Rumpal Stilts Kin*, a 'Dramatic spectacle', which was acted by members of the authors' families.[5] It would seem that Disraeli wrote the arias, songs and choruses of the work, none of which would have made many demands upon the artistic and literary temperament of an 18-year-old. For example:

> Music and wine
> To be divine
> The Gods owned long ago
> When they joyous quaffed
> The Nectar draught
> And blessed the genial flow.

One should not be too harsh on juvenilia, especially when the work under review was written, like *Rumpal Stilts Kin*, for family consumption only. Nevertheless, if one glances at these rhymes of 1823 (the one above is one of the more accomplished) and then reads *Vivian Grey* (1826), one cannot help feeling that Disraeli made a colossal improvement in his writing in the intervening three years. (*Rumpal Stilts Kin*, as can be seen from the subject matter in the rhyme above, was not written solely for children.)

With *Rumpal Stilts Kin* behind him, Disraeli began that same year his first attempt at a novel. Encouraged by his acquaintance with his father's literary cronies, he sent the manuscript in May 1824 to John Murray. The story was a satire on 'the present state of society' and told the adventures of a certain Aylmer Papillon in 'Vraibleusia'. If we consider that, in his nineteen years, Disraeli had hardly ventured outside Bloomsbury, we may also consider that a satire on 'the present state of society' was a trifle ambitious. Considering as well the merits of *Rumpal Stilts Kin*, it should be easy to see why Murray was not prompt in giving a verdict on the work. To give the young Disraeli his due, he was not so lacking in literary maturity that he did not soon recognise his own 'indiscretion'. Consequently, in the summer of 1824 he wrote again to Murray advising him to burn the manuscript, and there is no evidence to suggest that the publisher had any misgivings about following the young man's advice.[6] Disraeli left off attempting to write a novel for two years. As it happened, his first published work was not to be the sort of 'fiction' he had envisaged in 1824.

In fact, if that year produced any noteworthy writing by Disraeli, it was not to be found in any manuscripts for publication, but rather through his personal letters. At the end of July he went with his father on a six-week tour of Belgium and the Rhine Valley, and his letters home are full of colourful details about their travels and gourmandising. Robert Blake sums them up concisely from a literary point of view: 'The letters show a sharpness of observation and a satirical eye which anticipates the author of *Vivian Grey*. They also show much of the brashness, conceit and affectation which critics were to discern in the same work.'[7] Disraeli's imagination had been looking for room to expand and if the law office in Old Jewry was hard to bear before the summer of 1824, it was certainly intolerable after the Continental experience of the Rhine. By the beginning of 1825 Disraeli had turned his back on the law.

In Dickens's *Dombey and Son*, which was published in 1848, we are told by Miss Tox how Mrs Pipchin's husband broke his heart:

> 'In pumping water out of the Peruvian Mines...'
> 'Not being a Pumper himself, of course,' said Mrs. Chick, glancing at her brother; and it really did seem necessary to offer the explanation, for Miss Tox had spoken of him as if he had died at the handle; 'but having invested money in the speculation which failed.' (chapter 8)

Disraeli also did some pumping. If the enterprise did not kill him, it very nearly ruined him for life, and it did, in fact, leave him in a fragile financial state for many years to come.

Disraeli's involvement in speculation was characteristic of his approach to life in the 1820s; he acted on impulse with a vague notion of taking a short-cut to a position of power and money. The Spanish colonies of South America were in revolt. In England Canning was supporting the new republicans. Chaos and concessions led to an expansion of mining interests in these countries, and people rushed to invest in their continued growth. Most of the companies involved in the ex-colonies grew up out of the clamour, and many were a sham. But when the new republics were recognised by the British government just after Christmas 1824, success for the 'bulls' seemed assured. There was a boom, and many a Mr Pipchin hurried to invest his savings in pumping water out of Peruvian, Mexican and Columbian mines.

Before Christmas Disraeli had backed his instinct and speculated for the collapse of the mining companies. When the boom came he panicked and changed his tack. It was a mistake. The boom of mid-January was the high point of the shares; by spring the values were falling. By June 1825 Disraeli, with his two speculating partners, Evans and Messer, had lost £7,000. For Disraeli it was the beginning of years of money troubles.

If the speculation affected Disraeli's career as a novelist through the way it embarrassed him financially, it also gave rise to the occasion which brought about his first published work. Disraeli's involvement in the shares had brought him into contact with J. D. Powles, who was a partner in a firm of South American merchants. At Powles's instigation Disraeli wrote a pamphlet which propagandised the bullish views which were in the interest of the mining companies. This pamphlet, *An Enquiry into the Plans Progress and Policy of the American Mining Companies*, which masqueraded as a disinterested analysis of the situation by 'one whose opinions are unbiased by self-interest', ran to a hundred pages and was published by John Murray (who, it might be added, had himself money at stake in the shares) in March 1825. The merits and moral rectitude of the pamphlet are, of course, questionable. Not surprisingly, however, given the climate of feeling in England at the time, it sold well, going through several editions and being reviewed in the *Gentleman's Magazine* of May 1825.

Disraeli followed up this 'success' by writing two more anonymous pamphlets of a similar nature, both of which were as disingenuous and, given the flimsy nature of many of the mining companies, as irresponsible as the first. If the opportunism and flagrant self-interest of this enterprise betrayed the nascent politician in Disraeli, the pamphlets also represented a less than auspicious beginning for the career of a writer. His motives were clearly financial, but again we see the need to 'fictionalise' in his own self-interest.

Although by now Disraeli seemed to be committed to some kind of literary hack life, he was still intent on seizing the 'main chance' and acquiring influence through a flurry of youthful genius. His own ideas of power and fame were, in the 1820s at least, more important to him than the actual act of writing, and when, in 1825, John Murray gave him some basic literary work, like the preparation of the manuscript of a Life of Paul Jones, Disraeli carried out the task in a perfunctory manner, producing no prose of his own which was anything other than commonplace. There was, however, one 'project' in the back of John Murray's mind which Disraeli found of great interest: the idea of starting a new daily newspaper.

If, by 1825, the extreme financial and speculative optimism of the previous year was no longer at a peak, there was certainly still enough money and enthusiasm available to make almost any enterprise seem practicable. Such enthusiasm, in fact, masked some of the realities of the situation. Murray certainly seems to have been at least a little less than his usual self when he put forward the idea of launching a newspaper for which Disraeli (who, through his pumping of South American mines, had just lost his share of £7,000) was to contribute a quarter of the cost.

John Murray had been the moving spirit behind the founding of the *Quarterly Review* in 1809. Although never quite as successful as the *Edinburgh Review* (founded in 1802), upon which it was modelled and against which it was designed to compete, the *Quarterly* was nevertheless a successful publication, despite its obvious Canningite bias which rendered it often less than impartial as a critical organ. The two Reviews not only generated great enthusiasm in the political and literary arenas but they also dispensed considerable amounts of money and prestige for their writers and editors. Newspapers were altogether a different proposition. Sir Walter Scott was later to tell his son-in-law, John Gibson Lockhart, when the latter was editor of the *Quarterly*, that a connection with any newspaper would be 'disgrace and degradation'. Scott's opinion of newspapers may always have been the same, but certainly, by the time he wrote that comment to Lockhart, his view had been considerably reinforced by the fiasco surrounding the conception and birth of the paper which Murray had intended should challenge *The Times*.

It was Scott's celebrated son-in-law whom Murray had in mind as the guiding light of his new project, and in September 1825 Disraeli travelled to Scotland as emissary for the publisher, with the task of winning over Lockhart. Although Lockhart's reception of the young envoy was less than warm, Disraeli was introduced to Scott within a few days of his arrival, and one cannot help thinking that by that time the young man certainly considered himself to be in a world of fantasy based on political negotiation and peopled with eminent personages. He wrote to Murray in code, calling himself 'The Political Puck', and there is no doubt that, given the partisan nature of most major publications in the 1820s, Disraeli considered himself to be on a most political mission. He wrote saying that Lockhart must be convinced that 'he is coming to London, not be an Editor of a Newspaper, but the Directeur General of an immense organ, and at the head of high bred gentlemen and important interests'.[8] This must be kept in mind when we read *Vivian Grey*, because it would appear that even before Disraeli plunged into his first published novel, his mind was already 'fictionalising' the events concerning the establishment of the newspaper. His letters to Murray speak of organising a new political party, but there is no supporting evidence to suggest that this was anything other than a figment of Disraeli's active fantasising. Whether his imagination interfered with his mission or not, Disraeli certainly seems to have bungled affairs; Lockhart showed no interest in the proposed newspaper, so Murray (without Disraeli's assistance or hindrance) quickly brought him down to London with, instead, the offer of the editorship of the *Quarterly*.

Although the Lockhart incident came as a snub to Disraeli's own inflated idea of himself as a 'political' entrepreneur, he continued to regard his trip to Scotland as proof of his ability to influence the creation of political cabals. Once back in London he continued to hustle John Murray and others with his enthusiasm for the project but, as the paper became increasingly 'organised', Disraeli became more abstracted from the centre of activity. His last real contribution to its genesis was to christen it – the *Representative*. The paper was finally published on 25 January 1826 and was a disaster. After seven months, during which John Murray lost £26,000, it ceased publication.

The revised edition of *Vivian Grey*, which appeared in 1853, had a preface which contained the following remarks:

> Books written by boys, which pretend to give a picture of manners and to deal in knowledge of human nature, must necessarily be founded on affectation. They can be, at the best, but the results of imagination, acting upon knowledge not acquired by experience. Of such circumstances exaggeration is a necessary consequence, and false taste accompanies exaggeration...Such productions should be exempt from criticism, and should be looked upon as a kind of literary lusus.

By 1853 Disraeli was a front-bench politician and an ex-chancellor of the exchequer, and so it was to be expected that he would find *Vivian Grey* something of an embarrassment; if the revised edition could not wipe away the tone of youthful extravagance, it was at least able to exorcise the many solecisms of the original. It is, of course, true that Disraeli's experience was, in 1826, as in 1824 when he wrote *Aylmer Papillon*, limited; but it is not strictly correct to say that *Vivian Grey* was the result 'of imagination, acting upon knowledge not acquired by experience'. Disraeli may not have, in reality, rubbed shoulders with the aristocracy, nor have been the instigator of a new political party – but by 1826 he had certainly shown himself capable of transferring what experience he *did* have into a grander and more adventurous arena through the medium of his fiction.

By the end of 1825 Disraeli must have felt somewhat jaded by his efforts to secure the success of the *Representative* – and in as far as those efforts were abortive, he may have considered himself to have been thwarted and frustrated by the unconciliatory Lockhart and the less than clear guidance from Murray. If Disraeli's own literary nature and background were reason enough for him to begin a fresh attempt at a novel, that feeling was reinforced at the end of 1825 by a desire to withdraw, at least temporarily, from the hurlyburly world, and also a need of financial resources.

Withdrawal was achieved to some extent when Disraeli went to stay at Hyde House, near Amersham. Isaac D'Israeli had rented this country house for the autumn through the solicitor Benjamin Austen. The house belonged to Robert (later Plumer) Ward, a 60-year-old man who, earlier that year, had published his 'society' novel *Tremaine or the Man of Refinement*. Austen had acted for Ward by placing the book with the publisher Henry Colburn after the author's daughters had copied the manuscript in order to preserve the work's anonymity. Apart from the letting of Hyde House, the links between the D'Israelis and the Austens were close. Isaac, through Austen, had read the manuscript of *Tremaine* before it was published, while Benjamin quickly formed a relationship with Austen's wife, Sara, that was to be based on a combination of professional expediency and sexual attraction. It might also be added that, mainly through her persuasions, Austen became a considerable creditor of the young Disraeli over the next few years. Indeed, the childless Sara may well have fulfilled, either directly or indirectly, all of Disraeli's most pressing desires and needs.

By February 1826 Disraeli had finished the beginning of his novel, and he approached Sara in the hope that she would effect a process of submission and publication along the lines of *Tremaine*, upon which to some extent the new work was based. The difference between the emerging manuscript and *Aylmer Papillon* was considerable; recent experience had added a cogent subject matter and improved the style. After Sara had read this part of-the manuscript she wrote to Disraeli saying 'take me as an Ally *upon trust*',[9] and so started a process whereby she became amanuensis, agent and confidante for the new novel's advancement.

Sara's enthusiasm was stirred by her personal attachment to Disraeli, while his own excitement, fostered by his great vanity, grew out of the depression of the *Representative* affair. As publication became probable rather than just possible he threw himself again headlong into this fresh project. If the combined zeal of Sara Austen and Disraeli at any time threatened to dissolve the secrecy which it was intended should cloak the project outside the limits of the D'Israeli family, then certainly no such intoxicated enthusiasm was to be shown by the publisher chosen to be honoured with the manuscript.

Henry Colburn was a shrewd businessman. He was deemed to be the most appropriate man for Disraeli's new project for no other reason than that he had published *Tremaine* under similar circumstances of secrecy. He was no model of literary principle. As Michael Sadleir has described him, Colburn

> regarded every author as having his price and the public as gullible fools. He cared nothing about book-design, nothing about crafts-manship. Cheapest was best, so long as the leaves hold together . . . He had no literary taste of his own, merely an instinctive sense of the taste of the moment. In consequence . . . he published on the basis of quick turn-over, and made a fortune for himself by sheer topical ingenuity . . . Impervious to snubs; cheerful under vilification, so long as insults meant more business; thinking in hundreds where others thought in tens, Colburn revolutionised publishing in its every aspect . . . He developed advertising . . . to a degree hitherto undreamt of. He had his diners-out who talked up his books at dinner-tables and soirées; he debauched the critics and put them on his pay-sheet . . . He was a book-manufacturer, not a publisher.[10]

Such was the man who gave the unremarkable sum of £200 for the copyright of the new novel. Indeed, it seems likely that as his main aim was purely to make some quick money, one can gauge the amount of money paid to the author by the fact that Colburn probably laid out £100 or so for the advertising or 'puffing' of the work. Through his friends and partners he had a great deal of influence in the periodicals of the day, several of which he partly owned, and the puffs soon began to appear thick and fast. The *New Monthly* said: 'It is understood that nearly all the individuals at present figuring in fashionable society are made to flourish with different degrees of favour in the pages of the new novel.' The hero of the book, according to *John Bull*, was 'insidious, daring, decisive, anything but insipid'. The *Globe* claimed that 'probably there will scarcely be a single assembly of *haut ton*, public or private, from which *Vivian Grey* will be absent'. The *Sunday Times* and *Bell's Weekly* both spoke in terms of a 'political Don Juan', a phrase used by Vivian himself in the novel.

It is hardly surprising that fashionable London took Colburn's bait; through the machinations of his publisher Disraeli found himself about to be propelled anonymously into a glare of publicity. As soon as the novel appeared on 22 April 1826 it became an instant topic of conversation, as the many personages of Vanity Fair flocked to attempt to fathom the *real* identity of the novel's characters and its author. After all, Colburn had claimed that the author was 'a man of high fashion – very high – keeps the first society'.[11] The first mystery, however, was of as much consequence, and readers were 'aided' in their detections by the issuing of several keys to the characters. Disraeli may not have foreseen quite the way in which the novel would be 'sold' when he wrote it, but his vanity could not in any case have prevented him from enjoying the situation. He may have written *Vivian Grey* for fame, but in 1826 he was willing to accept the infamy.

Disraeli was still only 21 years old when *Vivian Grey* was published. In many ways it is characteristic of several 'first' novels by writers who are not great novelists; much of it is transcribed from letters and other literary sources (like the conversation about Byron), and some of the novel is tedious. It is not the aim of this book to promulgate the 'merits' of those passages of Disraeli's fiction which have rightly been ignored by literary critics. However, a discriminating eye can find much which is of interest for the idea of Disraeli's character and, from the point of view of *this* study, how that influenced his career as a writer of fiction.

Vivian Grey will probably always be regarded as that one of Disraeli's early works most worthy of scrutiny, and in the past that interest has focused mainly on the work as a form of autobiography. But as has been indicated, this aspect of the fiction, especially regarding the author's adolescence, will remain difficult to analyse until we possess more concrete evidence of Disraeli's childhood and, particularly, evidence of his relationship with his parents. Nevertheless, the opening of the novel has an undeniable zest and vigour which, whether justifiably or not, colours our interpretation of the author's life. The real sustaining feature, however, of *Vivian Grey* is the story of the intrigues and plans surrounding Vivian and the Marquess of Carabas.

As was obvious to several readers soon after the publication of *Vivian Grey*, the story is a thinly veiled interpretation of the events surrounding the founding of the *Representative*. Vivian Grey, a precocious, young, supremely confident and ambitious man, inveigles himself into the favour of the less than astute Marquess of Carabas. By a combination of flattery and intrigue he suggests to Carabas that the latter should assume again the mantle of power and prestige which was once his, through the formation of a new political party. Carabas takes the bait, and Vivian is sent off as an emissary of this nascent political group to secure the support of Frederick Cleveland, an erstwhile opponent of Carabas, but now the man adjudged most able to lead the new party.

At the beginning of the story the novel travels at a fast pace, held together by the wit and preciosity of the hero. Once out of London the unfolding of events becomes, if not more leisurely, at least more 'stagy', as the narrative is dilated with the round of dinner parties and new acquaintances associated with a stay at a country house. To cut a long story short, Vivian's well-made plans are torpedoed by the Marquess's sister-in-law, Mrs Felix Lorraine, and the unravelling of the complications leads eventually to the hero's killing of Cleveland in a duel. When he wakes up the next morning and realises what he has done, Vivian foams at the mouth and falls exhausted on his pillow. It is decided that he should go abroad for a while.

The similarity of this escapade to that surrounding the founding of the *Representative* hardly needs pointing out. People who were aware both of the newspaper fiasco and of the authorship of *Vivian Grey* could see the details plainly enough, as well as the way in which Murray and Lockhart were apparently portrayed in the characters of Carabas and Cleveland respectively. Such portrayals, especially in their caricatured forms, were much to blame for the ill-feeling which the novel engendered in the minds of men who, only a few months previously, had treated Disraeli as a confidential agent. Relationships were particularly soured between the D'Israelis and John Murray, who considered himself to have been grossly insulted by the scenes which showed him as a man who drank too much.

Interestingly, however, the similarities between Murray and Carabas as characters are virtually non-existent, and one must really consider whether Disraeli was perhaps not merely using the framework of the *Representative* story without paying too much attention to individual personalities. After all, once we have acknowledged the factual basis of the plot and characters, the interest lies more in the areas where Disraeli the novelist *departed* from historical events in his presentation. His reinterpretation here is a combination of fantasy, ambition and excuse. Where the original experience concerned a newspaper, this fictional parallel is the founding of a political party fit to assume the leadership of the country (an idea which, as we have seen, seems to have occurred to Disraeli while he was on his mission to Scotland). Where the original project was Murray's idea, the political initiative in *Vivian Grey* is wholly the brain-child of the hero. Whereas Disraeli's inexperience led him to bungle his wooing of Lockhart, Vivian Grey is only defeated by the Machiavellian intrigues of Mrs Felix Lorraine. And where Disraeli withdrew from the field sulkily to find solace with Mrs Austen and his writing, Vivian's surge for power climaxes with his own honourable conduct and the almost accidental killing of Cleveland.

What must be remembered, of course, is the fairy-tale element of much of what happens in the novel. When Disraeli introduces the Marquess to us at the very beginning of Book II, we are told, 'The Marquess of Carabas started in life as the cadet of a noble family. The earl, his father, like the woodman in the fairy tale, was blessed with three sons.' The reference is to the story of Puss in Boots, although in most versions the 'woodman' is, in fact, a miller. Briefly the story concerns a miller who, on dying, leaves his three sons his mill, his ass and his cat respectively. The youngest son feels hard done by and cannot see any merit in his legacy, the cat, save for the possibility of eating it and making a muff of its skin. The cat, however, thinks differently and, asking only for a bag and a pair of boots, tells the son that he will make his fortune for him. The cat, obviously endowed with a good deal of self-confidence, goes to see the king of the country, taking him presents of rabbits, partridges and the like, and saying that they are gifts from the marquis of Carabas – 'for that was the title he was pleased to give his master'.

By means of deception, the cat manages to convince the king that the miller's son is a very rich and great landowner. This deceit is aided when the cat kills the local ogre (who has conveniently taken on the form of a mouse), thereby making available a vacant castle for the 'marquis'. The king is so impressed by all this that he marries his daughter, the princess, to the marquis of Carabas. There is, of course, also ample reward for the cat; we are told that he 'became a great Lord, and never more ran after mice, but for his diversion'. The tale is mainly unusual in that the hero little deserves his good fortune, and George Cruikshank, who edited the story in the nineteenth century, took particular exception to 'a system of imposture being rewarded by the greatest worldly advantages'.[12] Certainly in this respect at least, the fairy tale was a perfect antecedent of *Vivian Grey*. Vivian's planned deception may not be ultimately as successful as the cat's, but both of them have the same basic aim in mind – survival and then self-aggrandisement.

The question remains as to how seriously we are meant to take the impulses and reactions which lurk under the fairy-tale-like construction. There seems to be too much absurdity in the tale for us to accept the bulk of it either as a frank recollection of past feeling, or as a provocative statement of growing ambition in a young man soured by recent criticism. The sense of humour too often departs from the ironic to indulge in a kind of perverse mockery. Of course, nothing Vivian says can really be taken out of his own schematic context, but, even so, when he talks to Julia Manvers on the subject of shooting, for example, we cannot help feeling that, through his hero's humour, Disraeli is pursuing the kind of tactics which led his father to speak in an uncomplimentary way of Miss Herschel's sex-life:

> No, I'm no shot; – not that I have not in my time cultivated a Manton; but the truth is, having, at an early age, mistaken my most intimate friend for a cock pheasant, I sent a whole crowd of *'fours'* into his face, and thereby spoilt one of the prettiest countenances in Christendom. (*Vivian Grey*, II, x)

It is the presence of passages like this that make it difficult for us to really see *Vivian Grey* as a 'society' novel. Indeed, Matthew Whiting Rosa, in *The Silver Fork School* (1936), said: 'To trace the connections between the first part of *Vivian Grey* and various literary precedents is possible but likely to be misleading, because the chief merit of the book is derived from its personal flavour.' It would seem true that the atmosphere surrounding Hyde House, Plumer Ward and Sara Austen was really all the precedent needed to explain the nature of Disraeli's first novel, both in its 'society' background, and in its appearance of self-analysis. In terms of this latter quality, a search for precise links with Byron and Goethe would seem to be a fruitless occupation; not only was their influence very diffuse by 1826, but, more important, Disraeli was mainly interested in reworking his own adventurous fairy tale in the terms of his idiosyncratic style.

'Society' as such for Disraeli was very much an agglomeration of those things which he associated with the external trappings and fittings of a rich life: exotic clothes, conspicuous jewellery, and, perhaps above all in this novel, food. It was the food which had so impressed him when he made his Continental trip with his father, and it was the instinct of the gourmet which came easily into his writing, investing it with a *real* sense of the 'silver fork'. From Antwerp he had written in his letters of

> A *fricandeau*, the finest I ever tasted, perfectly admirable, a small and very delicate roast joint, veal chops dressed with a rich sauce piquant, capital roast pigeons, a large dish of peas most wonderfully fine, cheese, dessert, a salad preeminent even among the salads of Flanders which are unique for their delicate crispness and silvery whiteness, bread and beer *ad lib.* served up in the neatest and purest manner imaginable, silver forks, etc.

And from Brussels he wrote to tell his sister that he had 'kept a journal of dinners for myself'.[13]

When Disraeli came to write *Vivian Grey* much of this instinct was transferred into the fiction. He complained about 'London dinners! empty artificial nothings!', while later he obviously felt that his role as narrator did not preclude him from the more interesting pursuit of recommending specific dishes to the reader (in one case, cabinet pudding with curaçao sauce). Food also attracted Disraeli because of its many comic possibilities. When Vivian interposes himself late at the table of one particular dinner, the chairs are moved along and all the guests are suddenly propelled down the table a distance of two feet:

> Dr. Sly, who was flourishing an immense carving-knife and fork, preparatory to dissecting a very gorgeous haunch, had these fearful instruments suddenly precipitated into a trifle, from whose sugared trellis-work he found great difficulty in extricating them; while Miss Gusset, who was on the point of cooling herself with some exquisite iced jelly, found her frigid portion as suddenly transformed into a plate of peculiarly ardent curry, the property, but a moment before, of old Colonel Rangoon. Everything, however, receives a civil reception from a toad-eater, so Miss Gusset burnt herself to death by devouring a composition, which would have reduced any one to ashes who had not fought against Bundoolah. (*Vivian Grey*, II, xiv)

It is this extravagant and over-rehearsed nature of the portrayal of 'society', rather than any knowing irony, which is central to Disraeli's 'adventure'. It threatens to induce in the reader not so much a sense of shared humour, as rather a slight hysteria. It is a world stage-managed to contain not only a glut of haunches, trifles and iced jellies, but also a fair share of gaudy decor and manic melodrama. We have the Marquess, leaning back in his chair with his eyes shut:

> In the agony of the moment, a projecting tooth of his upper jaw had forced itself through his under lip, and from the wound, the blood was flowing freely over his dead white countenance. (*Vivian Grey*, IV, iv)

Or Mrs Felix Lorraine:

> Her complexion was capricious as the chameleon's, and her

countenance was so convulsed, that her features seemed of all shapes and sizes. One large vein protruded nearly a quarter of an inch from her forehead; and the dark light which gleamed in her tearful eye, was like an unwholesome meteor quivering in a marsh. (*Vivian Grey*, IV, v)

The style has an undeniably engaging quality, but it also marks out its author to be a novelist limited by his own lack of restraint. It is too much an exercise in artificial extravagance, and its appeal is not so much that of a novel as rather that of a novelty. As the book moves towards its climax the 'drama' becomes more pronounced, as the 'elevation' of the hero requires continuous and outrageous stimulation. Horace Grey writes to Vivian,

You are now, my dear son, a member of what is called *le grand monde* – society formed on anti-social principles. Apparently you have possessed yourself of the object of your wishes; but the scenes you move in are very movable; the characters you associate with are all masked; and it will always be doubtful, whether you can retain that long, which has been obtained by some slippery artifice. Vivian, you are a juggler; and the deceptions of your sleight-of-hand tricks depend upon instantaneous motions. (*Vivian Grey*, III, viii)

The same may very well have applied to Disraeli. Midway through 1826 he was still, as far as most of the reading public was concerned, the anonymous 'man of high fashion'. But he was also conscious that, like Vivian Grey and Puss in Boots, he too, partly through the machinations of Henry Colburn, had become the perpetrator of a prime deception. The question remained as to what society's opinion of him would be once it had been revealed who the author was. The exposure of Disraeli the novelist was soon to come.

Notes: Chapter 2

1 Quoted by B. R. Jerman, *The Young Disraeli* (Princeton, NJ: Princeton University Press, 1960), pp. 87–8.
2 See W. F. Monypenny and G. E. Buckle, *The Life of Benjamin Disraeli, Earl of Beaconsfield*, 6 vols (London: John Murray, 1910–20), Vol. I, pp. 25–31.
3 Quoted by Robert Blake, *Disraeli* (London: Eyre and Spottiswoode, 1966), p. 19.
4 Quoted by Monypenny and Buckle, Vol. I, p. 37.
5 Published by The Roxburghe Club (1952) with an introduction by Michael Sadleir.
6 Fragments of the ms. remain: Disraeli Papers, Box 231.
7 Blake, p. 22.
8 Quoted by Blake, p. 28.
9 Quoted by Jerman, p. 51.
10 Quoted by Ian Jack, *English Literature 1815–1832* (Oxford: Clarendon Press, 1963), pp. 30–1.

11   Cyrus Redding, *Fifty Years' Recollections*, quoted by Lucien Wolf in his introduction to *Vivian Grey* (London: The De La More Press, 1904), p. xli.

12   Quoted by Iona and Peter Opie, *The Classic Fairy Tales* (1974), London: Book Club Associates/Oxford University Press, pp. 110–16.

13   Quoted by Monypenny and Buckle, Vol I, pp. 44–5.

3

Rivers of Diamonds

In March 1868, when Disraeli was Prime Minister and Gladstone was leader of the Liberals, the following piece appeared in the *Pall Mall Gazette*:

> One of the most grievous and constant puzzles of King David was the prosperity of the wicked and the scornful, and the same tremendous moral enigma has come down to our own days...Like the Psalmist, the Liberal leader may well protest that verily he has cleansed his heart in vain and washed his hands in innocency; all day long he has been plagued by Whig Lords and chastened every morning by Radical manufacturers; as blamelessly as any curate he has written about *Ecce Homo*; and he has never made a speech, even in the smallest country town, without calling out with David, How foolish am I, and how ignorant! For all this, what does he see? The scorner who shot out the lip and shook the head at him across the table of the House of Commons last session has now more than heart could wish; his eyes, speaking in an Oriental manner, stand out with fatness, he speaketh loftily, and pride compasseth him about as a chain...That the writer of frivolous stories about *Vivian Grey*...should grasp the sceptre before the writer of beautiful and serious things about *Ecce Homo* – ...is not this enough to make an honest man rend his mantle and shave his head and sit down among the ashes inconsolable?[1]

The fact that *Vivian Grey* could still be held, albeit wittily, against Disraeli when he was Prime Minister, says a lot for the feelings that the novel engendered when it was published more than forty years before. The fact that several accounts of Disraeli's life have based many assumptions on his supposedly reckless and insincere character has its origin to a great extent in the aura which grew up around the young novelist. That reputation dogged Disraeli for longer than his lifetime. The view that he was an unprincipled schemer is as unsupportable as it is distasteful. Daniel O'Connell's taunt that Disraeli was a 'living lie' oversimplified the character of a man who allowed his imagination to actively elaborate on everyday life.

A month after *Vivian Grey* had appeared it was still popular to speculate as to who the author might be. Magazines and papers like the

Star Chamber, the *Globe* and *John Bull* variously suggested identities for the secret personage. Those suggestions included John Wilson Croker, who was, among other things, a close friend of Robert Peel; Theodore Hook, a novelist and editor of *John Bull*; William Maginn, a notorious and less than sober Irish journalist; the Hon. Anthony Ashley, the son of the Earl of Shaftesbury; Plumer Ward; and even Lockhart himself.

The matter was as frivolous as it was investigative. While Lord Normanby spent his time by writing to newspapers to deny any connection with *Vivian Grey*, Lord Glengall was confessing to the authorship. Such absurd diversity could not ensure the anonymity for long. Sara Austen was soon writing to Disraeli to tell him that his own name had been mentioned in connection with the novel by William Jerdan, the editor of the *Literary Gazette*. Jerdan had already made the point, in fact, in his review of *Vivian Grey* which appeared on 22 April, that the figure behind the novel was more likely to be a literary man than he was a fashionable gent. As he said: 'The class of the author was a little betrayed by his frequent recurrence to topics about which the mere man of fashion knows nothing and cares less.'[2] By June Disraeli had been exposed. For the time being the air of frivolity and wit could continue, as in *John Bull*:

> Mr. Samuel Rogers having stated the fact that the entertaining novel of VIVIAN GREY was the production of D'Israeli, his friend exclaimed – 'Indeed! are you sure?' – ''*Tis really*,' said the wag. It may be as well to add to this *witticism*, that *young* MR. DISRAELI is the author of the novel, and not his father, as some people have imagined.[3]

Such 'witticism' was not, however, typical of the public reaction to the discovery of the author. The general feeling was one of outrage at the imposture, and this outrage was stoked by the deep resentment with which much of the literary establishment regarded Colburn. The result was to be a chastening experience for the young novelist.

In many respects the furore of the critics was aimed at the publisher of *Vivian Grey*; it was, after all, his publicity which had originally captivated the ever-present audience of sycophants. The literary world was not a forgiving world either, and there were many journalists and reviewers who had cause to be embittered against Colburn on old accounts. As has already been said, however, Colburn was 'Impervious to snubs, cheerful under vilification, as long as insults meant more business'. He was much too thick-skinned to respond to accusations of 'puffery' and imposture. The most vulnerable target, therefore, was the author, and it was Disraeli who bore the brunt of the attack.

The foremost members of this offensive were the *Literary Magnet* and the *Monthly Magazine*, both of which were spurred on by a hatred of Colburn and his own ring of influence in literary circles. The *Magnet* published a so-called *Secret History of Tremaine and Vivian Grey*, which accused Sara Austen of defrauding Colburn, and Disraeli of basing his novel on a diary he had stolen from Plumer Ward. Predictably the affair of the *Representative* was dragged up and distorted. In the *Monthly Magazine* George Croly, the Irish poet and novelist, declared *Vivian Grey* to be

> immeasurably the most impudent of all feeble things, and of impudent things the most feeble; begot in puppyism, conceived in pertness and born in puffing. Whether the writer was anything above a collector of intelligence in servants' halls and billiard rooms, no one, of course, could tell, for no one had ever heard his name before; but the graces of a tavern waiter and the knowledge of a disbanded butler, are but sorry things, after all, to trade upon; and this miserable product of self-sufficiency was received with the contempt due to its abortiveness.[4]

The review ended by saying that Disraeli's 'only chance of escaping perpetual burlesque is to content himself with sinking into total oblivion'. 'We shall probably', he added, 'never have to mention his name again.' A month earlier *Blackwood's* had published the suggestion that *Vivian Grey* had been written by 'an obscure person for whom nobody cares a straw'. Infamy Disraeli may have been able to bear, but the idea of being ignored was a severe blow.

In order to recover somewhat from the exhaustion and exposure of notoriety, Disraeli left England in August 1826 for a tour of the Continent with the Austens. Even this 'escape' was fated to be a trip heavily flavoured with literary romanticism, for in Geneva he met Byron's boatman, Maurice, who had rowed the poet out on the lake during the great storm described in *Childe Harold's Pilgrimage*:

> How the lit lake shines, a phosphoric sea,
> And the big rain comes dancing to the earth!
> And now again 'tis black, – and now, the glee
> Of the loud hills shakes with its mountain-mirth,
> As if they did rejoice o'er a young earthquake's birth.

Disraeli had Maurice row him out on to the lake evey night, and while the writer sat waiting for a thunderstorm, the boatman would relate stories about Byron. In the end Disraeli had to settle for just the lightning: 'It was sublime – lightning almost continuous, and sometimes in four places, but as the evening advanced the lake became quite calm, and we never had a drop of rain.'[5]

From Switzerland Disraeli and the Austens crossed the Alps into

Italy, finally returning home through France. In all, the tour had only lasted two months, but as far as Disraeli was concerned it seemed to have achieved its purpose. He arrived back in England in the autumn refreshed and excited. Far from being still depressed over his literary baptism, he had engaged himself during much of the tour in writing a sequel to *Vivian Grey*. Once home, he again embarked on a frantic programme of writing in order to get it finished as soon as possible. Indeed, the speed of composition may well have been enlivened by the thought of a substantial payment. After all, if he was going to be burdened by a certain reputation anyway, he might as well make some money from it; Disraeli still had some considerable outstanding debts, including one to John Murray. Henry Colburn obliged by paying the sum of £500 for the sequel, which was more than twice as much as the original had earned its creator. It was a generous payment for a book which did not have the feverish appeal of its predecessor. The author of *Ecce Homo* only got around to reading it when Disraeli was Prime Minister, and his concise opinion then of the book as 'trash' is not one which could easily be argued against.

As the work was nearing completion, the original novel was going into its third edition in a rather pruned form. Elaboration was no less a part of Disraeli's art, but excess extravagance had to be curtailed, and readers of the third and subsequent editions were to be denied some of the gourmandising spirit to which attention has already been drawn:

> What a dull dinner! I have eaten of everything: – *soup printannière* (twice) – fillets of turbot *à la crême* – fowl *à la Montmorenci*, garnished with *ragout à l'Allemande* – neck of veal *à la Ste. Menehoult* – *marinade* of chickens *à la St. Florentin* – *Muriton* of red tongue, with spinach – six quails – two dishes of kale, merely with plain butter – half a dozen orange jellies, *en mosaïques* – cauliflowers with *velouté* sauce, and a *petit gateau à la mae non* – a *soufflée* with lemon, and a dozen Neufchâtel cheeses – a bottle of Markebrunnen, a pint of Latour, and a pint of Maraschino. Gone through it all; and yet here I am, breathing as freely as a young eagle. Oh! for an indigestion, if merely for the sake of variety! (*Vivian Grey*, IV, ii)

While such pieces had been cut out with a mixture of expediency and the genuine regret of an indiscretion, Colburn's organs were at work enhancing the chances of a similar 'fame' for the sequel. The *New Monthly Magazine* said: 'The continuation of *Vivian Grey* will speedily appear. The author will not be turned from the career of his humour by the pitiful snarlings which have lately wounded him', and the *Globe* declared that 'Curiosity is highly excited respecting the contents of the forthcoming volumes of this piquant work'.

The final three volumes of the novel appeared on 23 February 1827. If the reviews were still not generous, they were, at least for the most part, free of the acid invective which had greeted the revelation of the author's identity. After what had been two years of almost continual activity, Disraeli collapsed with exhaustion. It was to be more than three years before he was fully well again.

Disraeli had not really set out to be a novelist. His ideas concerning his future career were vague. What seems certain is that *Vivian Grey* grew out of a mixture of frustration, fun, financial peril and Disraeli's ever-present thirst for fame. It was not undertaken as a conscious first step towards the life of a novelist, and it seems unlikely that the merits or the reception of *Vivian Grey* were of a kind to persuade Disraeli that his future lay in fiction. As has been suggested already, Disraeli *did* have a luxuriant and ever-active imagination – but these 'qualities' are by no means a qualification or a justification for writing. Considering *Vivian Grey* was Disraeli's first novel, conceived largely as an elaborate prank, and then plumped out with the gobbets of an undigested fancy, its 'success' was no mean feat. If, in retrospect, while Disraeli languished, plagued with 'chronic inflammation of the membrane of the brain', the memory of *Vivian Grey* equalled little more than a loss of anonymity, then that did not seem a bad thing. It was too early, of course, for him to appreciate what real damage such a reputation might do.

If there was an immediate lesson to be learnt from *Vivian Grey* it surrounded the presentation of *real* people and events under thinly veiled 'fictional' equivalents. Disraeli had no regrets as far as the portrayal of such people as Lockhart was concerned, and the depiction of the *Representative* affair through the story of the Marquess of Carabas was at once an effective poke at Murray and also a defence of Disraeli's own conduct in the business. Nevertheless the book had made him enemies.

Disraeli's ambition seemed to lie not in any specific direction but rather in a general yearning for power and influence. As it turned out, of course, this desire was to find eventual satisfaction in politics – but politics, in the late 1820s, was by no means so distinct a field of action for Disraeli as it was to become in the following years. Whatever the 'chronic inflammation' may have been, it certainly did not help to clear the occasional mist from the mind that could dream at once in terms of social, political, literary and even religious leadership. In his more level-headed moments, however, Disraeli realised that his best hope of achieving any sort of influence was by ingratiating himself with 'society' – even if the role he was to play had already been cast as that of a 'bête noir'. It was possible, although not easy, to make the transference through literary fame from bookish drawing rooms to elegant and brilliant salons. If such a transference required the right acquaintances as well as the right books, Disraeli could at least acknowledge that society was there to be cultivated. It was both a more likely and enjoyable way of achieving influence than either an ascetic application to literature, or an immediate and unsupported offence on the hustings. For the time being political principles might be a matter of theory and expediency. 'Literature' could at once serve the need for myth, money, glamour, the recasting of experience and the recording of experiments.

The lesson of *Vivian Grey* therefore seemed clear enough. The impact on society must be retained – but personal caricature was something to be used with more discrimination. The titillation of public taste and vanity was acceptable, but the burlesquing of those persons who might be of some use in climbing the ladder of success was obviously not politic. If, during 1828, Disraeli's illness forced on him an uncharacteristic despondency as regards his ability to climb that ladder, it only led to a sharpening of will and purpose in the years immediately following. The mining speculation, the *Representative* affair and *Vivian Grey* had caught Disraeli up and whirled him on the wheel of life at a pace which suited his ambition but not his constitution. What was needed was a degree of calculation that would control, but not mute, the energy and idiosyncratic application which had marked the last three years.

When Disraeli next took up his pen it was for exercise and experiment. In 1828 a small novel, *Popanilla*, appeared. It was a more mature dash at the topic which had formed the core of the manuscript which John Murray had burned four years before. This time Disraeli's satire on society was founded more on a knowledge of affairs, and from poking fun at the Utilitarians, the work fans out to cover many of the facets of English public life which Disraeli, in the 1820s, found exasperating. (Interestingly the Corn Laws come in for a share of his satire.) However, the scale and tone of the book must be kept firmly in mind. *Popanilla*, rightly, caused little stir when it was published, and only partisan readers saw in it anything of lasting literary merit. Plumer Ward, for example, wrote that 'Since the days of Swift and Voltaire I have not read anything so witty. Je riais aux éclats and made others do so too. In my opinion it is equal to the *Tale of a Tub* and *Candide*, and superior to *Zadig* and *Babouk*.'[6] A brief glance at Disraeli's work would reveal the over-exuberance of such a comparison. In itself it is satire at its most contrived, but it does show us how Disraeli was widening his grasp of literary method. Although there is little ground for claiming in *Popanilla* a portent of Disraeli's Young England novels, the work was certainly a worthwhile exercise, and one in which we can glimpse a flexing of the author's muscles.

With his health still a cause for concern, Disraeli was soon to have the chance to acquire some real and local physical exercise. Isaac

D'Israeli finally forsook his corner of Bloomsbury, and the family moved out to a house a few miles from High Wycombe. Bradenham was to be the home of Isaac for the rest of his life and the constant autumnal retreat of Benjamin while he remained a bachelor. Over the next few years he was to become a keen walker in the surrounding countryside, as he strove first for fitness, and then for votes.

By the autumn of 1829 Disraeli's health was returning, and with a new lease of life his imagination again darted off into the realms of fantasy and adventure. This time it was the mystic East which fascinated him, and, as was often the case, the infatuation found expression in both literature and action. For over a year, it seems, Disraeli had been toying with the idea of writing a novel about the Jewish hero, David Alroy, and if he had been an author motivated purely by artistic ambition, then it seems likely that an Eastern romance would have been his next publication and expression of his roving ideal. But the lure of the East was not for Disraeli a simple literary lure to be nurtured on research and invention. He also desired to visit Jerusalem. And why stop there? He quickly convinced himself that what was needed was a grand tour of the Mediterranean and the Near East. It was, after all, an excursion which could be excused on the basis of his own health.

The problem was, hardly surprisingly, money. If imagination was the spur to Disraeli's literary pursuits, money was the bridle, and no less important in deciding the direction in which the fiction would progress. Thus it was that the ideas surrounding David Alroy were shelved, and Disraeli took up his pen with the precise aim of producing the kind of novel which would appeal, albeit in a more discriminating way, to that section of the public that had clamoured for *Vivian Grey*. As he told Benjamin Austen in December 1829:

> I fear I must *hack* for it. A literary prostitute I have never yet been, tho' born in an age of general prostitution & tho' I have more than once been subject to temptations which might have been the *ruination* of a less virtuous young man. My mind however is still a virgin, but the mystical flower, I fear, must even be plucked – Colburn I suppose will be the bawd. Tempting Mother Colburn![7]

By 14 February 1830 Disraeli had decided to forgo the professional services of Sara Austen and was himself making an initial approach to Colburn:

> I have been fool enough to be intent upon a novel. But such a novel! It will astound you, draw tears from Princesses, & grins from Printers devils: it will atone for all the stupid books you have been lately publishing, and allow me to die in a blaze. In a word to give you an idea of it. It is exactly the kind of work which you would write

yourself, if you had time, and delightfully adapted to the most corrupt taste. This immortal work which will set all Europe afire & not be forgotten till at least 3 months has only one fault, – it is not written.[8]

Volumes I and II were, in fact, finished and by the end of March Colburn had agreed to publish the work. The state of the book trade at that time was depressed. This meant that Disraeli was unable to get an offer of more than £500 from his publisher, and it also meant that the appearance of the book was to be delayed for a year. Such a predicament forced Colburn to be more than usually careful, and he told Disraeli that his reader acknowledged the novel's 'amusing extravagance which will cause it to be read but at the same time he adds that it is certain of being *seriously criticised* for its egotism & other sins of the writer!' By this time the state of the market had also obliged Colburn to take on as a partner his printer, Richard Bentley, and on 17 May Disraeli decided to settle for what he could get and signed an agreement with the two of them. He received an immediate payment of £400 in postdated bills, with the prospect of another £100 on the publication of a second edition. He was to write to his sister: 'I don't care a jot about *The Young Duke*. I never staked any fame on it; it may take its chance.' With the money in hand Disraeli had achieved his purpose in writing the book; two weeks later he was on his way east.

The winter of 1829/30 was also notable in that it marked the beginning of Disraeli's friendship with Edward Lytton Bulwer. In his diary for 1833 Disraeli wrote:

I have not gained much in conversation with men. Bulwer is one of the few with whom my intellect comes into collision with benefit. He is full of thought & views at once original and just.[9]

It would appear that their acquaintance began in 1829 with an exchange of letters. By early 1830 they had met and found each other's company mutually agreeable. By April Bulwer was reading *The Young Duke* in manuscript, and his remarks to Disraeli on the subject are most illuminating:

I could fill my letter with praises of its wit – the terseness & philosophy of its style – & the remarkable felicity with which you make the coldest insipidities of real life entertaining & racy ... In the genius of your book I see not a flaw, nothing to point out to your attention. In the judgement of it, I think you are less invariably happy. – You do not seem to me to have done justice to your own powers, when you are so indulgent to flippancies ... The flippancies I allude to are an ornate & shewy effeminacy that I think you should lop off ... To a mere fashionable novel aiming at no higher merit, & to a mere dandy aiming at nothing more solid, the flippancy ... might be left, & left gracefully. But I do not think the one suits a man who is capable of great things nor the other a man who occupies great places... You have attained in the Book more than the excellencies of Vivian Grey, but I do not think you have vigilantly enough avoided the faults.[10]

Disraeli was disheartened by Bulwer's remarks, which were directed against the first two-thirds of the novel. Whether or not Disraeli sensed this apparent fault himself, the latter parts of *The Young Duke are* muted in terms of glittering flippancy. To some extent this may have been due to Disraeli's admiration of Bulwer even before they met. The latter's successful novel *Pelham* (1828) had adhered to the formula whereby society was first portrayed in all its splendour (a style which implicitly ridiculed its subject), while the latter parts of the book descended into a darker and lower world from which the hero could rise morally and politically regenerated. *The Young Duke* itself is a tale of lustrous degeneration, followed by moral redemption for its hero, the Duke of St James, and through the pattern of redemption Disraeli makes the point (which was to be so important to his later novels), that the aristocracy must learn to recognise its moral and political responsibilities. To some extent the early flippancies in the novel are therefore not all as disposable as one might think, and although Disraeli considered the work to be a prostitution of his abilities, it shows how much he had matured since *Vivian Grey* in his depiction of excess and its consequences.

It is another example of the author's imagination at work; but here we *are* forced to make a distinction. Robert Blake has made the point that imagination 'is not the same as fantasy or day-dreaming. The capacity to invent characters, to get inside them and present their development, the power to put oneself into unfamiliar scenes and situations, everything that is meant by creative imagination, was not Disraeli's *forte*.'[11] As we have seen, Disraeli's imagination very much depended on fantasy and day-dreaming; it was a manipulative imagination rather than a creative one, and it throve on the author's own infatuations. Those infatuations have always been the subject of comment by biographers, but it remains an interesting question as to how Disraeli used such fetishistic sensibilities in his work as a novelist. André Maurois, one of Disraeli's most sympathetic biographers, wrote:

> he found pleasure in describing receptions of royal splendour, regiments of footmen liveried in scarlet and silver, tables laden with gold-plate, rivers of diamonds on the necks of women, ancestral sapphires and rubies darting their sombre fires.[12]

Such pleasure shows an addiction to glamour, but what is interesting is how such a glamour was portrayed. There is a passage in *The Young Duke* where the narrator says:

I find this writing not so difficult as I had imagined. I see the only way
is to rattle on just as you talk. The moment you anticipate your pen in
forming a sentence, you get as stiff as a gentleman in stays. I use my
pen as my horse; I guide it, and it carries me on.

It would seem that this might well reflect the way in which Disraeli was
wont to write, especially considering the rushed and prostituted
circumstances surrounding *The Young Duke*. Even so, it would appear
that Disraeli was still capable of endowing his early fiction with
imaginative strains which would back up the story or theme. Bulwer
may well have been right to pick on Disraeli's habit of indulging in
flippancies, but the author of *Vivian Grey* was now also able (perhaps
not consciously) to use those excesses to forward his design.

The Young Duke certainly portrays a society of dazzling brilliance,
which is mainly noteworthy for the amount of light it generates to shed
upon itself. The people in the novel are all 'brilliants', and the parties
they attend 'so numerous . . . that the town really sometimes seemed
illuminated'. In fact, the superlatives are heaped up in such a fashion
that the splendour becomes the norm, and everything that does not
have that peculiarly eye-catching quality is deemed a flat failure. It is
through this world that the Duke of St James passes, sparkling on from
one excess to another. If the rich personages, dripping in finery,
resemble a *jeunesse d'orée* or god-like members of some *beau monde*
pantheon, it is considered only fitting. They are the bright stars in
whose glow the lesser lights cluster. When it is pointed out to the Duke
that he is being stared at, he says (taking his cue partly from *Henry IV,
Part One*, I, ii): 'we were made to be looked at. 'Tis our vocation, Hal,
and they are gifted with vision purposely to behold us.'

The Duke, however, is himself stunned by the radiant beauty of May
Dacre, who is a veritable beacon: 'She turns her head, she throws
around a glance, and two streams of liquid light pour from her hazel
eyes.' Indeed, Miss Dacre is so luminous that on her nearly all jewellery
is superfluous, and so light that we are left in doubt as to whether her
delicate body is a fitting place for crustaceous gems: 'she wore, indeed,
no necklace; with such a neck it would have been sacrilege; no earrings,
for her ears were too small for such a burthen'.

However, only May is endowed with such qualities. Everyone else in
Disraeli's society shows a distinct reliance on jewellery. It is only
through jewellery, we are made to feel, that most of the aristocrats
manage to catch the eye of the beholder. Only by gems can they
impress. Only by carrying about on their person such polished prisms
and pieces of light-catching metal can they maintain their lustrous
exteriors in a world of competitive show and extravagance. People in
The Young Duke are measured by their jewels, and their ornamental
riches are a sign of their power. This may seem an obvious statement

(i.e. power equals money), but Disraeli is not quite so blunt. *His* jewels are splendid ornaments in a sense which is almost divorced from money itself. A person in *The Young Duke* is esteemed not merely because his or her jewels represent monied wealth; that person is esteemed because he or she is lit up like a Christmas tree.

It is only, then, a slight extension of this when Disraeli talks about people themselves as jewels. Even May Dacre cannot escape this process: she 'was a jewel set in gold, and worn by a king'. The Duke of St James enters society 'having been stamped at the Mint of Fashion as a sovereign of the brightest die', and he is 'flung forth, like the rest of his golden brethren, to corrupt the society of which he was the brightest ornament'. There is a certain noble simplicity in this; in contrast, many of the diamond-spattered dowagers seek to achieve a more crusted state – more akin to that of walking candelabra.

Under such a weight of decoration it is understandable that questions of physiognomy are subsumed in the greater theme of *bijouterie*; the two daughters of the Countess of Fitz-pompey 'were as much like their mother, as a pair of diamond ear-rings are like a diamond necklace'. The Duke of St James's personal jeweller, Mr Garnet, even employs a bejewelled idiom in his speech; when told by the Duke to keep a secret, he says, 'as for myself, I am as close as an emerald in a seal-ring'. The extreme is attained by a certain Count Frill, who 'was all rings and ringlets, ruffles and a little rouge'. One has the impression that were this young studded buck to be accosted and stripped of all his alliteration, nothing would be left. The rings have supplanted the hands, the ringlets the head, the ruffles the body and the rouge seems a sad apology for the face.

It is fitting, then, that Disraeli makes this jewellery, this icing on his roué's cake, central to the Duke of St James's relative decline:

> He discovered that in the course of two years he had given away one hundred and thirty-seven necklaces and bracelets; and as for rings, they must be counted by the bushel. The result . . . was, that the Duke had not only managed to get rid of the immortal half million [his inherited fortune], but had incurred debts or engagements to the amount of nearly eight hundred thousand pounds, incumbrances which were to be borne by a decreased and perhaps decreasing income. (*The Young Duke*, IV, ix)

The question comes back to financial resources in the end. But, even so, Disraeli still makes us feel that the Duke is to be pitied more because he is no longer at the point of dispersal for such a shower of decorative wealth. The fact that the gems and 'the immortal half million' are one and the same is not always obviously before us, so distinct seems the unworldly, fairy-like realm of carats.

From this point on the novel significantly pays far less attention to jewellery. From this point on the Duke, in crude terms, has learnt his lesson. He realises the true worth of 'esteemed' society and, having given away so many jewels, he is left, fortunately, with May – the one self-generating girl who does not need such artificial knick-knacks. The 'rivers of diamonds' in *The Young Duke* are therefore not only part of the novel's décor; they form a series of images which support the author's theme, and as such they contribute something to our understanding of Disraeli's imagination.

In many respects, however, *Contarini Fleming* and *Alroy* were Disraeli's two most important early novels. But neither could have been written if it had not been for his tour of the Near East which must be seen as both an extension of the young man's former dreams and also as an important influence on his later ideals. As with the tour of the Rhineland with his father, and the Alpine excursion with the Austens, Disraeli has left us a permanent record of the details of travelling and sojourning in the many letters he wrote.[13]

He left London by steamer on 28 May 1830 and arrived in Gibraltar a month later. He was travelling with William Meredith, the friend of the family who had collaborated on the writing of *Rumpal Stilts Kin* and who was now engaged to be married to Disraeli's sister, Sarah. The landing of Disraeli at Gibraltar was something like the arrival of a celebrated novelist. As he wrote to his father at the beginning of July, *Vivian Grey* was regarded by the inhabitants of the rock

> as one of the masterpieces of the nineteenth century. You may feel their intellectual pulse from this. At first I apologized and talked of youthful blunders and all that, really being ashamed; but finding them, to my astonishment, sincere, and fearing they were stupid enough to adopt my last opinion, I shifted my position just in time, looked very grand, and passed myself off for a child of the Sun just like the Spaniard in Peru.[14]

The child of the sun and his companion travelled on horseback through Andalusia, before returning by sea to Gibraltar at the end of July. By the end of August they were in Malta where they met an old friend, James Clay. As with the trip to Switzerland, this tour was bound to resurrect Disraeli's interest in Byron, and the young novelist was delighted to find that Clay had in his service the poet's former manservant, 'Tita' Falcieri. During September the three young men left Malta in Clay's yacht, *The Susan*, and sailed first to Corfu, and then on to Yanina, which was the capital of the Turkish province of Albania. A combination of romantic recklessness and a crusading spirit had given Disraeli notions of joining the Grand Vizier's Turkish army which was engaged at the time in putting down the Albanian revolt of 1830. It is perhaps fortunate that the travellers arrived too late for any pseudo-military exploits, although the Grand Vizier did receive them in some style. As Disraeli wrote to Austen on 18 November:

> For a week I was in a scene equal to anything in the Arabian Nights – such processions, such dresses, such corteges of horsemen, such caravans of camels – Then the delight of being made much of by a man who was daily decapitating half the Province.[15]

From Albania they travelled to Navarino, Corinth, Argos and Mycenae, arriving at Athens on 24 November. From there they sailed for Constantinople, where Disraeli and Clay remained enchanted for six weeks, although Meredith left them halfway through December to explore Asia Minor. They all met again in Smyrna, and then while Meredith scurried off again to see 'the unseen relics of some unheard-of cock and bull city' Disraeli and Clay went on to Jaffa, and from there to Jerusalem. Disraeli spent a week in Jerusalem – a week that he called 'the most delightful in all my travels'.

By 12 March 1831 the two travellers were in Alexandria, and after meeting Meredith again, Disraeli decided to remain several months in Egypt, visiting Cairo and Thebes. By the end of June his thoughts were returning homewards, and the three men began to make plans for their return journey. It was then that tragedy struck. Meredith contracted smallpox and died on 19 June. The news completely stunned the inhabitants of Bradenham, and Disraeli left the East immediately to be with his sister.

The death of his prospective brother-in-law forced Disraeli to put to the back of his mind, at least temporarily, the dream he associated with the mystic East. He was once more back in polite English society, and determined to use his position to its full advantage. The main thing in his favour in his assault on society was his friendship with Bulwer. Although Disraeli was far from being sought after by the leading lights of the brilliant society he had already portrayed with a combination of scathing criticism and envy, he *did* become a regular guest of such ladies as Lady Blessington, Lady Cork and Mrs Norton. Disraeli's cultivation of this section of society was the result more of his extra-ordinary manners than of his novels, and he wallowed in the spirit of dandyism which suffused the parties of Alfred, Count d'Orsay, who lived with Lady Blessington. Disraeli's interests and emotions were far too eclectic and unpredictable for him to have fully emulated d'Orsay, and he developed his own brand of extravagance which depended as much on his idiosyncratic tastes as it did on the vogue of dandyism. Society seems to have been sometimes bemused and sometimes infuriated by Disraeli's failure to fit into any well-defined category. While his literary opportunism rendered him something less than a gentleman of fashion, his society pretensions, and his evident lack of interest in other writers (with the notable exception of Bulwer), together with his past embroilments, caused him to be taken none too seriously by much of the literary world.

But, important as society was to the young Disraeli, it was not the only thing of importance. His imagination and fancy was still restless, creating and re-creating worlds within which he could excel. No less concerned with ideals and mysteries, Disraeli began to explore the tangible possibilities for political advancement. It was at this time that he produced what he always considered was his best novel – his Psychological Auto-Biography.

Just when exactly the Psychological Auto-Biography was written we cannot be sure. The preface to the 1845 edition claimed that the work had been composed 'in a beautiful and distant land'. Indeed, it does seem likely that the novel was conceived at least during the tour of the Near East, and literary and historical comparisons would support the view that it was the product of the same mixture of idealism and introspection which had given rise to the first plans for the story of David Alroy. However, important as the tour was in forming the spiritual atmosphere for the work, and necessary as it proved regarding the provision of wide-ranging descriptions, the new book could also be seen as a conscious rebellion against the 'rivers of diamonds' and the circumstances which had forced Disraeli to write *The Young Duke*. It is a lucid, albeit flowery at times, assertion of his own idiosyncrasies, and through its frequent affectations we can glimpse facets of the Disraelian personality which complement and extend our picture of the mind which wrote *Vivian Grey* and *The Young Duke*.

Disraeli's confidence in his own creation was one of the reasons why, in February 1832, he approached John Murray with the manuscript. Seven years had elapsed since the *Representative* fiasco, and the best that could be said of the relationship between Disraeli and the publisher was that it was businesslike. It is perhaps strange that Murray sought Lockhart's opinion of the work. Not surprisingly, Scott's son-in-law felt he could say little on the subject, and so Murray asked the poet and historian, Henry Hart Milman, to read the manuscript. The reader's response was enthusiastic, and he told the publisher that not only was the work a 'very remarkable production', but that it was 'a "Childe Harold" in prose'. Milman foresaw the work being much read, much admired and much abused, although both he and Murray disliked the idea of publishing it as *A Psychological Auto-Biography*. Instead, they suggested using the name of the hero as the title of the book, and the work became known as *Contarini Fleming*.

Disraeli objected to the change, saying later that the novel had been published 'under the bibliopolic baptism of "Contarini Fleming", which means nothing'. But he was really in no position to argue. He had put as much store by the novel's financial expectations as he had by what he felt would be its imminent literary reputation, and so the author contented himself with having the work subtitled 'A Psychological Auto-Biography'. Murray, like most publishers, was suffering a depression in his business and, although Milman's recommendation was a strong one, Disraeli could not afford to be obstructive. His original offer to Murray was to let the publisher have the four volumes for an advance of £200, but when the wary Murray suggested instead that the work should be published at half-profits, Disraeli accepted. The deal did Disraeli's insolvency problems very little good. Murray ran off 1,250 copies and *Contarini Fleming* appeared in the middle of May. Unfortunately for all concerned, not least Disraeli's creditors, only 614 copies were sold. When the final profits were worked out, Disraeli found himself better off by £56.

B. R. Jerman sums up the situation well when he says that 'the reading public is always much more interested in reformed young dukes than in pathological poets'.[16] For the majority of readers weaned on *Vivian Grey* and *The Young Duke*, *Contarini Fleming* was notable only for its lack of wit and exuberance. Yet for the modern reader, the Psychological Auto-Biography is a prime example of Disraeli's character. Here we see again the practised interpreting of events and emotions; but, with concern much more focused on a commitment to 'seriousness' and the individual's strength of character, the overall impression is one of a mind which was not only idiosyncratically reformist, but also revolutionary.

Early in the novel Disraeli establishes his tone of earnestness:

> I am desirous of writing a book which shall be all truth, a work of which the passion, the thought, the action, and even the style, should spring from my own intellect, from my own observation of incident, from my own study of the genius of expression...I have resolved therefore to write the history of my own life, because it is the subject of which I have the truest knowledge. (*Contarini Fleming*, II, i)

Set against this is the warning that Christiana gives the hero: 'Ah! Contarini, beware of your Imagination.' The continual piling up of such references is one of the indications of a new kind of self-consciousness in the stance of Disraeli as narrator – a self-consciousness heightened, of course, by the first-person narrative. Yet it is also a style which threatens often to parody itself and the author. After Contarini has won the prize for his essay, he recalls: 'I was not less self-conceited or less affected, than before, but my self-conceit and my affectation were of a nobler nature.' Vivian Grey might have thrown off such a comment with a wry smile, but in *Contarini Fleming* Disraeli is purposely eschewing witticism in an attempt to be both sincere and experimental. As has already been suggested, Disraeli's sincerity is not necessarily lessened by the way his mind elaborated on reality. In calling his work a Psychological Auto-Biography, with a 'created' hero, he was allowing himself the luxury of overtly fictionalising his own life, and it is interesting to see how his interpretive imagination worked on experience, especially in those areas of education and writing which have concerned us so far.

For example, Disraeli's hankering regrets about his own education and his feeling that he was now making a conscious contribution to English literature combine when he has his hero declare:

> Even as child, I was struck by the absurdity of modern education. The duty of education is to give ideas. When our limited intelligence was confined to the literature of two dead languages, it was necessary to acquire those languages, in order to obtain the knowledge which they embalmed. But now each nation has its literature, each nation possesses, written in its own tongue, a record of all knowledge, and specimens of every modification of invention. Let education, then, be confined to that national literature, and we should soon perceive the beneficial effects of this revolution upon the mind of the student.
> (*Contarini Fleming*, V, xxi)

Of course, the parts of the book which most clearly parallel Disraeli's feelings on writing itself are those which deal with the composition and reception of *Manstein*, the novel which Contarini writes in a flurry of authorship. An obvious difference in the parallel of *Manstein* and *Vivian Grey* is that, whereas Disraeli was almost a nobody when he wrote his first novel, Contarini Fleming is already a politician and a member of government. After what we have seen of Disraeli's active imagination, especially during the *Representative* affair, it is easy to see why extravagant and perhaps premature advancement features so strongly in this Auto-Biography. In Contarini's case, *Manstein* is not strictly his first publication. The prize-winning essay already referred to, written at college, 'was printed, lavishly praised in all the journals, and its author, full of youth and promise, hailed as the future ornament of his country'. Disraeli notably allows his hero a more auspicious literary baptism than that he had experienced with his mining pamphlets.

With the relation of the *Manstein* affair, Disraeli combines this extravagance with a certain new awareness and frankness. Where the composition of *Vivian Grey* had been quick, the writing of *Manstein* is quicker:

> I took up a pen. I held it in the light. I thought to myself what will be its doom, but I said nothing. I began writing some hours before noon, nor did I ever cease. My thoughts, my passion, the rush of my invention, were too quick for my pen. Page followed page; as a sheet was

finished I threw it on the floor; I was amazed at the rapid and prolific production, yet I could not stop to wonder. In half a dozen hours I sank back utterly exhausted, with an aching frame. I rang the bell, ordered some refreshment, and walked about the room. The wine invigorated me and warmed up my sinking fancy, which however required little fuel. I set to again, and it was midnight before I retired to my bed.

The next day I again rose early, and with a bottle of wine at my side, for I was determined not to be disturbed, I dashed at it again. I was not less successful. This day I finished my first volume. (*Contarini Fleming*, II, xii)

Contarini is aware that his work is based on 'fancy', and he soon realises that 'In depicting the scenes of society in which my hero was forced to move, I suddenly dashed, not only into slashing satire, but even into malignant personality . . . Never was anything so imprudent.' The imprudence of the work is what occasions the eventual torrent of abuse when the identity of the author is discovered. However, far from being in a situation where any critic might call the author 'an obscure person for whom nobody cares a straw', Contarini exudes an air of adventure and quiet understatement:

I found even a strange delight in being an object, for a moment, of public astonishment, and fear, and indignation. But the affair getting at last troublesome, I fought young De Bragnaes with swords in the Deer Park, and having succeeded in pinking him, it was discovered, that I was more amiable. (*Contarini Fleming*, II, xv)

The wit of *Vivian Grey* seems close at hand here, although Contarini goes on to claim his great serious intention as a writer:

I buried my face in my hands. I summoned my thoughts to their last struggle. I penetrated into my very soul, – and I felt the conviction, that literary creation was necessary to my existence, and that for it I was formed. (*Contarini Fleming*, II, xv)

Contarini Fleming, of course, has the luxury of being able to turn his back on a government post, and it would be difficult to say with any precision how far this 'conviction' reflected Disraeli's thoughts at any time between 1826 and 1833. *Vivian Grey* is in many ways a more 'political' novel than anything else Disraeli fictionalised before his Young England days, and it is perhaps strange that at a time when politics was about to become his main interest, he chose to write what is arguably his most disinterested book. Disraeli wrote in his diary a few years later that he would always consider *Contarini Fleming*

as the perfection of English Prose, and a Chef D'oeuvre. It has not paid its expenses. V[ivian] G[rey] with faults which even youth can scarcely excuse, in short the most unequal, imperfect, irregular thing that indiscretion ever published has sold 1000^S & eight years after its public[ati]on a new edit: is announced to day – So much for public taste!

If some parts of *Contarini Fleming* seemed to pledge Disraeli to the life of an author, others suggested quite the opposite. On his appointment to the government of his country, Contarini says:

> So much more impressive is Reality than Imagination! Often, in reverie, had I been an Alberoni, a Ripperda, a Richelieu; but never had I felt, when moulding the destinies of the wide globe, a tithe of the triumphant exultation, which was afforded by the consciousness of the simple fact, that I was an Under Secretary of State. (*Contarini Fleming*, II, xi)

Later Contarini realises that Imagination is not divorced from reality. Even after a bout of successful diplomacy he can say: 'In imagination I shook thrones and founded empires. I felt myself a being born to breathe in an atmosphere of revolution.' Behind what may now appear a commonplace Wordsworthian sentiment lies an indication of a mind which was growing to be not merely deft and interpretive in expression, but truly radical in intention.

Notes: Chapter 3

1   *Pall Mall Gazette*, 3 March 1868, quoted by W. F. Monypenny and G. E. Buckle, *The Life of Benjamin Disraeli, Earl of Beaconsfield* (London: John Murray, 1910–20), Vol. V, p. 3.
2   Quoted by B. R. Jerman, *The Young Disraeli* (Princeton, NJ: Princeton University Press, 1960), p. 65.
3   Quoted in ibid., p. 65.
4   Quoted by Lucien Wolf in his introduction to *Vivian Grey* (London: The De La More Press, 1904), p. xlviii.
5   Letter to Isaac D'Israeli, quoted by Robert Blake, *Disraeli* (London: Eyre & Spottiswoode, 1966), p. 52.
6   Quoted by Monypenny and Buckle, Vol. I, p. 120.
7   Quoted by Jerman, p. 91.
8   Quoted by Charles C. Nickerson in 'Disraeli's *The Young Duke*', *The Disraeli Newsletter* (published by the Queen's University at Kingston, Ontario), vol. 3, no. 2 (Fall 1978), p. 19.
9   Quoted by Nickerson, p. 25.
10 Quoted in ibid., p. 26.
11 Robert Blake, 'Disraeli the novelist', *Essays by Divers Hands* (1966), p. 14; quoted by Nickerson, p. 32.
12 André Maurois, *Disraeli*, trans. Hamish Miles (London: Bodley Head, 1927), pp. 41–2.
13 See Monypenny and Buckle, Vol. I, pp. 136–80.
14 Quoted by Blake, pp. 60–1.
15 Quoted by Jerman, p. 114.
16 ibid., p. 150.

4

Fortune and Fancy

When, on 30 August 1841, Sir Robert Peel became Prime Minister, Disraeli hoped to be among those Tories appointed to positions within the government. It was with the aim of securing a post that he wrote to Peel asking the Prime Minister to recognise his ability and character. This was not the only letter to recommend the services of Disraeli. Another appeal claimed that 'Literature he has abandoned for politics. Do not destroy all his hopes, and make him feel his life has been a mistake.' The writer of the letter was Disraeli's wife, Mary Anne. By 1841 Disraeli had done more than get married. He had also become a back-bench Tory MP of some repute, and among his varied writings were three more novels. In fact, since the publication of his Psychological Auto-Biography a great deal had happened in Disraeli's life. In some ways the years between 1832 and 1841 seemed to forewarn of a diminution in his appetite for 'fiction', and Mary Anne's remark is usually regarded as generally true. But those years also marked a time of such fervent and diverse activity in Disraeli's life that it would perhaps be surprising if his image as a novelist did *not* suffer in comparison with his emerging role as a politician.

Disraeli first met Peel in 1832 at about the time that *Contarini Fleming* was published. The meeting took place at a dinner party, after which Disraeli wrote to his sister Sarah:

> I can easily conceive that [Peel] could be very disagreeable but yesterday he was in a most condescending mood and unbent with becoming haughtiness. I reminded him by my dignified familiarity both that he was an ex-Minister and I a present radical.[1]

Disraeli may have conceived of himself as something of a revolutionary in 1832, and to some extent such an assessment could have justifiably been based on his own idiosyncratic mind. But although there is reason to believe that Disraeli's later political ideas were already forming themselves in that mind, his assertion in 1832 that he was a 'present radical' was really no more than an admission that, by virtue of his individualistic and non-aligned political campaigning, he was to be grouped with the band of eccentrically motivated independents who were a recognised part of pre-Victorian 'radicalism'.

It was as such a radical that Disraeli stood for election twice during 1832 at High Wycombe, and, at this stage of his political career, it would not be cynical to say that the basic desire to be in Parliament was far greater than the belief in, or the promulgation of, any particular ideology. An added spur was the fact that Bulwer had won a seat the previous year, and Disraeli could be forgiven for thinking that, even without a cogent political philosophy, his own mixture of talents could not fail to benefit the House of Commons. Expediency, however, demands that, at certain points in a career, colours of some kind be nailed to the mast, and such an act of impalement became increasingly necessary as Disraeli began to be accused not only of non-alignment, but also of (to use one of his own favourite words) tergiversation. It would hardly be flippant to suggest that Disraeli's considered opinion (if he had one) of tergiversation was equivocal. But, even if pragmatism were to be accepted as a constituent part of a politician's mind, it was obviously dangerous to acquire a reputation for adventurism and lack of principle. It was partly this reasoning which led him, in 1833, to publish a pamphlet called *What Is He? by the author of Vivian Grey*. As far as any practical political philosophy is concerned, the work tends towards the formation of a 'national' party; from the point of view of this study, however, what is as interesting is the fact that the publication should have drawn attention to *Vivian Grey*. If the quest for parliamentary fame was to begin with an attempt at respectability of purpose, such an attempt could not darken the basic sense of adventure which coloured all Disraeli's enterprises.

Those enterprises were not entirely political. If the public at the time of *What Is He?* needed any further reminding of the author's career in fiction, such a reminder was there in the shape of *The Wondrous Tale of Alroy* which was published in March. As we have seen, Disraeli had been contemplating an Eastern romance soon after the completion of *Vivian Grey*. If the idea for the book lay in his youth, then certainly it was also written in the same spirit that produced *Contarini Fleming*. To this extent, appearing in 1833, it represented a backward glance at the ideals and ambitions which had gnawed at Disraeli before the onset of his practical political endeavours, and it has been argued by some critics that *Alroy* was a watershed in his career as a novelist. Such a view, however, does not always help our understanding of him as a writer, even though it is a view which Disraeli himself helped to foster in the much-quoted words which were written in his diary in 1833:

> Poetry is the safety-valve of my passions, but I wish to *act* what I *write*
> – My works are the embodification of my feelings. In Vivian Grey I

have portrayed my active and my real ambition. In Alroy, my ideal ambition. [*Contarini Fleming*] is a development of my poetic character. This Trilogy is the secret history of my feelings – I shall write no more about myself.

To a large extent Disraeli was right in that his novels after *Alroy* were not built around obvious projections of his own ambitions. But, at the same time, the claim that 'I shall write no more about myself' over-simplifies his view towards 'fiction' during the years 1834 to 1847. There is no reason to think that such a claim, made in the privacy of what (for lack of a better word) we have called a 'diary', is anything less than sincere. Yet, once again, it stands as an example of the way in which Disraeli retrospectively sought to give form and purpose and direction to parts of his life which were more often dictated by fortune and fancy. The quantification and qualification of 'This Trilogy' therefore exists both as an example of Disraeli's perspicacity and as a trait of his habitual emphasis on life interpreted according to a plan of action.

Whatever the direction of Disraeli's ambitions as a writer in 1833, he was still faced with the practical problems of having *Alroy*, or for that matter any other work, published. He may well have been on his way to fame or infamy, but that did not disguise the fact that his past novels had not been notable for their financial success. As he sought a publisher for his Eastern romance he found the road closed to his most 'enthusiastic' advocate. Colburn had fallen out with his new partner, Bentley, and was temporarily out of business. Disraeli's other main contact also proved to be of no use, for John Murray feared another flop like *Contarini Fleming*. So it was that Disraeli was forced to find new sponsors, and they emerged in the form of Messrs Saunders and Otley. Whether or not they were flattered to receive this author's atten-tion, certainly by November 1832 Disraeli had secured what can only be called a generous advance of £300, considering the sales of *Contarini Fleming*. It was a sign of Disraeli's almost perpetual finan-cial embarrassment that even such an advance was completely swallowed up by an outstanding debt to Benjamin Austen. Such were the inauspicious events surrounding the publication of what Robert Blake has called 'perhaps the most unreadable' of Disraeli's romances.[2]

It would hardly be an exaggeration to say that the novel is not one which would recommend itself to anyone other than a devoted student of Disraeli. In its simplest form the story is that of a twelfth-century Jewish prince, his rise to spiritual and temporal power, his military conquests and his ensuing corruption which results from his (event-ually) misdirected ambitions. While it can be appreciated that such a narrative indulged what were, by then, the familiar, albeit fantastic, dreams of the author, it is the style of the writing itself which is mainly responsible for the reputation which *Alroy* has acquired. To be fair to Disraeli it must be pointed out that such a style was a conscious experiment, and moreover an experiment to which the author drew attention in the preface. If nothing else, the argument is direct:

> And now for my style. I must frankly confess that I have invented a new one. I am conscious of the hazards of such innovation, but I have not adopted my system without long meditation, and a severe examination of its qualities.

After such a revelation he then goes on to quote at length from *Contarini Fleming* the passage which declares that the age of versification is past. This is then reinforced by the claim that verse is 'essentially limited in its capacity of celebration', and, having prepared the way, he finally approaches an explanation of what is involved in the new style he has 'invented':

> As for myself, I never hesitate, although I discard verse, to have recourse to rhythm whenever I consider its introduction desirable, and occasionally even to rhyme. There is no doubt that the style in which I have attempted to write this work is a delicate and difficult instrument for an artist to handle. He must not abuse his freedom. He must alike beware the turgid and the bombastic, the meagre and the mean. He must be easy in his robes of state, and a degree of elegance and dignity must accompany him even in the camp and the market-house. The language must rise gradually with the rising passions of the speakers, and subside in harmonious unison with their sinking emotions.

It is perhaps a sufficient comment on Disraeli's stylistic explications that such passages were omitted from later editions of the novel's preface. In its defence, idiosyncrasy of character is no excuse for bad writing, but it does add a more interesting dimension to the prose than does an abortive attempt at literary theory. With some parts of *Alroy* the 'experiment' seems, indeed, to have run amok, and at such times one cannot help echoing the words of Rabbi Maimon (VI, iii) when he says, on the subject of 'the treatise of the learned Shimei, of Damascus, on "Effecting Impossibilities"', that 'The first chapter makes equal sense, read backward or forward'. In an attempt to highlight this aspect of Disraeli's authorship, one example must suffice:

> The water column wildly rising, from the breast of summer ocean, in some warm tropic clime, when the sudden clouds too well discover, the holiday of heaven is over, and the shrieking sea-birds tell a time of fierce commotion, the column rising from the sea, it was not so wild as he – the young Alroy.

Pallid and mad, he swift upsprang, and he tore up a tree by its lusty roots, and down the declivity, dashing with rapid leaps, panting and wild, he struck the ravisher on the temple with the mighty pine. Alschiroch fell lifeless on the sod. (*Alroy*, I, ii)

A recent critic of Disraeli, Daniel R. Schwarz, has said of the writing of *Alroy*, that 'Lyric interludes, sometimes in rhyme, certainly contribute to Disraeli's efforts to create an ersatz orientalism based on artifice rather than mimesis'.[3] While there is, of course, a good deal of truth in this, concerning Disraeli's *efforts*, such a statement seems less than frank in its endeavour to assess enthusiastically the author by his own standards.

Whatever one's view of stylistic adventurism, however, surely no one would deny the fact that the wordiness of *Alroy* dampens any response we might have both to the story and to the light the novel casts on Disraeli's interpretation of his own worldly situation. While the plot careers along a course which would have been highly acceptable to some of the early movie moguls, Alroy interjects pleas from his own conscience which give the novel a moral context. For example, early in the novel he cries out: 'Oh! this contest, this constant, bitter, never-ending contest between my fortune and my fancy!' On its simplest level of interpretation, Alroy's longing for a reconciliation of his fortune and his fancy is a projection of Disraeli's own desire to overcome his practical disadvantages by his dreams of heroism and advancement. It was a facet of his character which was complicated (notably by his own attempts to express it), and *Alroy* as a whole is hardly a coherent exposition of his dilemma. Nevertheless, Alroy's brief and extravagant career is an attempt to work through a moral problem in an off-beat artistic fashion, and Schwarz is probably right when he says that 'If Contarini vacillates erratically between imagination and action, Disraeli shows in *Alroy* that the life of action is not incompatible with the imaginative life'.[4] Such an acknowledgement of compatibility was to be of immense importance when Disraeli came, in the 1840s, to marry his politics with his fiction.

The moral perspective of *Alroy* is perhaps more pointed than in any of Disraeli's previous works of fiction. The abstraction of the world of the novel into an alien culture helps to give the author a certain freedom in the delineation of both character (such as it exists in Disraeli's work) and social trappings. But at the same time we never lose sight of the fact that the action of the story depends almost solely on the moral uprightness of its hero. It is noticeable that Disraeli, at this time, was also more obviously aware of the sexual tensions involved in a 'moral' life, and, despite *Alroy*'s apparent stylistic faults, the novel is important as a progression from what we have already seen to be Disraeli's idiosyncratic use of social décor. If it is a subject which demonstrates Disraeli's wit and joy of composition, rather than any didactic purpose, it is no less a facet of his creative process which demands some close attention.

The quotation used earlier from André Maurois to isolate Disraeli's use of jewellery extends to include a reference to what we have already seen was his considerable appetite for sumptuous food:

> he found pleasure in describing receptions of royal splendour, regiments of footmen liveried in scarlet and silver, tables laden with gold-plate, rivers of diamonds on the necks of women, ancestral sapphires and rubies darting their sombre fires, exquisite dishes, carriages laden with oranges and pineapples...and ortolans...It was only fitting that a dandy should cultivate his palate. One more conscious frivolity.

That such an indulgence as an ortolan is a legitimate detail for a critic might perhaps be supported by a reference to John Carey's perceptive and amusing discussion of a passage from Thackeray's *Memorials of Gormandizing.*[5] Carey, reviewing the remembrance of a Thackerayan meal, or rather the desecration of a 'poor little partridge', makes the interesting point that Thackeray's writing 'taps, through food, a reservoir of sensuousness which would have been unthinkable in the Victorian period, had he dealt directly with sexual experience'.

Disraeli's early novels were, of course, written during years very different from what we now associate with the words 'Victorian period'. He was, however, almost an exact contemporary of Thackeray, and although Disraeli was never able to compete with the author of *Vanity Fair* in writing or eating, they were certainly both concerned with the same English society. The ability to get behind and below the routine of everyday life and habits was a feature of Thackeray's work. It was also a quality which complemented and enhanced the witty and frivolous aspects of Disraeli's art. If *The Young Duke* highlighted a moral question through jewellery, it was also able to express a sensuousness through food:

> Ah, how shall we describe those soups, which surely must have been the magical elixir! How paint those ortolans dressed by the inimitable artist, à la St. James, for the occasion, and which look so beautiful in death that they must surely have preferred such an euthanasia even to flying in the perfumed air of an Ausonian heaven!
>
> Sweet bird! though thou hast lost thy plumage, thou shalt fly to my mistress! Is it not better to be nibbled by her than mumbled by a cardinal? I, too, will feed on thy delicate beauty. Sweet bird! thy companion has fled to my mistress; and now thou shalt thrill the nerves of her master! Oh! doff, then, thy waist-coat of wine-leaves, pretty rover! and show me that bosom more delicious even than

woman's. What gushes of rapture! What a flavour! How peculiar!
Even how sacred! Heaven at once sends both manna and quails.
Another little wanderer! Pray follow my example! Allow me. All
Paradise opens! Let me die eating ortolans to the sound of soft music!
(*The Young Duke*, I, x)

Of course, the Disraeli tongue must have been far into the Disraeli
cheek when he wrote this, and it might indeed be seen as a 'conscious
frivolity'. Nevertheless, the piece does harbour a witty seriousness
which conveys the passage's sensuousness. Passing over the sickly
humourous suggestion that the birds would have preferred euthanasia
to any form of paradisaical life, we find that the ortolans have assumed
a state akin to that of sexual go-betweens. Through the ortolan the
writer can imagine being nibbled by his mistress, while he faints away
into a rapturous appreciation of 'that bosom'. The eating of the small
bird evokes a degenerate luxuriousness that, in terms of digestion, is
almost debauched.

When Disraeli came to write *Alroy* he was interested not so much in
the way corruption was inherent in society and its trappings, as rather
the way in which the hero would have to maintain (or not) a moral ideal
glimpsed at the very beginning of the work. Among Alroy's
temptations is the sexual one, and in Schirene, the Gentile Princess of
Bagdad, the author created a woman who at times approaches a sexual
awareness which plays almost no part in Disraeli's other women. She is
given to violent jealousy, but her more subtle abilities for titillation are
conveyed in a more covert manner:

> Her attention was then engaged with a dish of those delicate ortolans
> that feed upon the wine-leaves of Schiraz, and with which the
> Governor of Nishabur took especial care that she should be well
> provided. Tearing the delicate birds to pieces with her still more
> delicate fingers, she insisted upon feeding Alroy, who of course
> yielded to her solicitations. (*Alroy*, IX, ii)

Although this is only one detail, the technique is one used both
generally in Disraeli's early novels, and particularly in *Alroy*. But
sexual response plays an important part in this novel, and affects the
'action' in a way that had not happened in any of the other works. It is
perhaps tempting to think that Disraeli, acknowledging that his created
world was exotically removed from the strictures of English society,
chose in *Alroy* to play with the idea of how sexual temptation might
affect both one's fortune and one's fancy. It was a subject which was
soon to engage his attention in a very real way.

It would probably be fair to say that, between 1833 and 1836, Disraeli's
life was dominated by love. It was during those years that he had his

passionate affair with Henrietta Sykes, a demanding and possessive woman, as can be seen from her letters to him. The illicit affair (Henrietta was, of course, married to a Berkshire baronet, Sir Francis Sykes) has been well chronicled by Robert Blake[6] and there is no reason here for restating the various stages of the relationship which began in the spring of 1833. It is of some importance though that, after his two election campaigns of 1832, the following year proved to be marked mainly by political inaction on Disraeli's part. This was a reflection of the state of the country as far as parliamentary aims were concerned, but such inactivity added to the way in which the new love affair swelled out to fill his day-to-day existence. He wrote on 1 September 1833 'I have passed the whole of this year in uninterrupted lounging and pleasure',[7] and, as such conditions were likely to be conducive to the exercising of Disraeli's idealising imagination, one is inclined to agree with Blake's assessment of the affair with Henrietta:

> it is possible to suspect that even from the start [Disraeli] was less in love with her than with the idea of being in love and being loved. A grand passion was an inseparable part of that Byronic tradition which so often sounds, with a slightly hollow note, in Disraeli's life.[8]

Fancy feeds on indolence, and Disraeli's months of lounging, together with his 'grand passion', conspired to awaken in him a new literary enterprise. We have already remarked on 'tergiversation' and how it seems to have been a favourite word of Disraeli's. It would appear that his own changeableness in the 1830s was due not so much to any original insincerity, but rather to a sometimes misplaced and wandering enthusiasm. Thus it was that, having claimed in his last two novels that the age of versification was past, he now decided to write an epic poem.

A great poem needs a great subject, and so the revolutionary in Disraeli decided that his epic would be about the French Revolution. He may well have visualised this as a sublime project which would have complemented his romantic relationship with Henrietta, but the combination of muse and mistress was not to be a felicitous one. Henrietta proved to be a distraction rather than an inspiration, and the epic progressed at a pace more leisurely than seemed fitting for such an earnest project. If one of Disraeli's eyes was on posterity, however, the other one was on the dunning letters which had become an habitual part of his life, and with the object of helping the financial situation, he directed some of his energy into a new novel. With the hope of regaining some of the popularity lost through *Contarini Fleming* and *Alroy*, and with the relevant experience near at hand, Disraeli launched himself into a love story. Halfway through, however, it was put aside; the epic was to get priority, and the epic plodded on. By early 1834 the great work, christened *The Revolutionary Epick*, was nearing completion. The first book was published in March, and the second and third books followed together in June.

If the combination of poetry, passion and illicit love fulfilled on one level Disraeli's yearning for 'that Byronic tradition', with *The Revolutionary Epick* he saw himself following in a tradition to which even Byron could not have pretended. It is no wonder that Disraeli's preface to the *Epick* has received more attention than the verse itself:

> It was in the plains of Troy that I first conceived the idea of this work. Wandering over that illustrious scene, surrounded by the tombs of heroes and by the confluence of poetic streams, my musing thoughts clustered round the memory of that immortal song, to which all creeds and countries alike respond, which has vanquished Chance, and defies Time. Deeming myself, perchance too rashly, in that excited hour a Poet, I cursed the destiny that had placed me in an age that boasted of being anti-poetical. And while my Fancy thus struggled with my Reason, it flashed across my mind, like the lightning which was then playing over Ida, that in those great poems which rise, the pyramids of poetic art, amid the falling and the fading splendour of less creations, the Poet hath ever embodied the Spirit of his Time. Thus the most heroick incident of an heroick age produced in the *Iliad* an Heroick Epick; thus the consolidation of the most superb of Empires produced in the *Aeneid* a Political Epick; the revival of learning and the birth of vernacular genius presented us in the *Divine Comedy* with a National Epick; and the Reformation and its consequences called from the rapt lyre of Milton a Religious Epick.

Disraeli rounds off this literary excursion by placing himself firmly in the tradition of Homer, Virgil, Dante and Milton, and announces that 'For me remains the Revolutionary Epick'. If his fancy did indeed struggle with his reason, it would seem that the former triumphed in this particular project. Yet again we can see, particularly in the excerpt quoted from the preface, Disraeli's unrelenting effort to categorise a literary and heroic tradition within which he might place himself. Such an effort was not a narrow process; it tailored itself to his whim (as we can see in his differing views on 'versification'), and it expansively included any tradition which might have appeared relevant. As has been suggested, the fancy did mask a 'revolutionary' tendency, the genuineness of which is not in question; the doubts expressed at the time concerned not Disraeli's role as a radical, as rather his pose as a poet.

Considering Disraeli had already tried to assert his political ambitions through the practical process of election, it is perhaps surprising that his literary energy was not partly channelled into some reflection or recountal of such an embroilment. However, if in the past literary historians have had no reason to question Disraeli's failure to chronicle an election, there has emerged recently evidence that he did 'fictionalise' such an event. It now appears that Disraeli was co-author of a novel which was published under pseudonyms at the same time as *The Revolutionary Epick*. The fact that we know anything at all about this novel is entirely due to the investigations made by the Disraeli Project.[9]

In the newsletter which the Project issued in Autumn 1979, principal investigator John Matthews outlined the discovery:

> Put simply, we have found, through following clues provided by the letters [of Disraeli], that Benjamin and Sarah Disraeli co-authored a novel in two volumes under the pseudonyms 'Cherry' and 'Fair Star', called *A Year at Hartlebury, or the Election*, which was published in London in March 1834 by Saunders and Otley. Most of the second volume, the detailed account of a borough election, is obviously by Disraeli, and equally obviously is based on his experiences in the two 1832 Wycombe campaigns.

The fact that only scholarly investigation could uncover this work is partly due to Disraeli's apparent failure ever to mention the book overtly. Such a fact alone is perhaps reason enough not to consider *Hartlebury* in the same light as Disraeli's other fictional enterprises. Nevertheless, in a study of this kind, the work offers, if not a reservoir of well-researched material, at least one more titillating perspective on this most idiosyncratic of authors.

It would seem that Sarah Disraeli was mainly responsible for the first volume, which opens innocently enough:

> Gentle reader, wander with us awhile, along the banks of this tranquil river, as it winds its course through this verdant valley, and we will show you a fair scene.
> Behold a rural green, encircled by cottages, and embosomed in wood-crowned hills. Each humble dwelling stands in the midst of a garden rich in vegetable store, and gay with the many-coloured tulip, and the golden crocus, and its slanting thatch is covered with the fragrant honeysuckle. It is the month of May, the air is filled with sweet odour and wild music. Hark! the clear note of the blithe Cuckoo, and ever and anon from yonder rich stack yard which surrounds that substantial looking farmhouse many a cheerful sound breaks on the ear. The green gradually ascends the side of the narrow valley, and, on the right on a sloping lawn, gay with laburnums, lilacs, and syringa, stands a low irregularly built house with gable ends and tall chimnies. It is the Parsonage . . .

By the end of the novel, however, Disraeli was probably the driving force of the partnership, spurred on both by his anonymity and, more important, by what must have been his desire to get the experiment over and done with. Chapter xvi of the second volume, ironically called 'A Friendly Conversation', contains a display of dastardly villainy which is almost bewildering, and a short while later a body is found horribly murdered in a ditch. As we see two of the locals descend from their knacker's cart to discover the corpse, we feel a long way from the garden of 'laburnums, lilacs, and syringa'. One of them, one Jin Flag, opines 'Murder will out . . . he could not have done it himself' – an astute remark concerning a body which has been shot in the back. It would appear fairly obvious who the murderer was, but Disraeli, possibly seeing the benefit of combining his own indifference with an air of mystery, did not feel the need for a condemning postscript of nemesis. The mystery remains, and the novel ends.

What gives *Hartlebury* its main interest, however, is obviously the description of the canvassing and election which takes up 164 pages of the second volume. It is here that we can see the undiluted Disraeli at work. The opening pages of this section of the novel are, indeed, rife with anti-Whig invective, which it may have been impolitic to publish under his own name. Interestingly, despite the broadsides aimed at the Reform Act (which, in the light of *Coningsby* and *Sybil*, we would expect from Disraeli's fiction), the novel's main character, Aubrey Bohun, bases his contempt of the Whigs on his feeling that they stand for the 'dismemberment of the Empire'. The likely conclusion to be drawn from such statements of anti-Whiggism in isolation is that Aubrey Bohun is a thinly disguised portrayal of Disraeli himself. And there are grounds for such an assumption when we meet the character. In a passage in Chapter xiv of the first volume, which was probably written by Sarah, we are told that

> Aubrey Bohun combined a fine poetical temperament, with a great love of action. The combination is rare. He was a man of genius. But with great powers he possessed what does not always fall to the lot of their possessors, – a great destiny. If a theory hitherto erroneous, had induced him to waste his youth in what some would style unprofitable and unsatisfactory pleasure, but which he would define as that unbounded pursuit of experience without which no powers are available; so fortunate was his lot in life, that at this moment with energy unsubdued though matured, a career was at his command in which he might redeem those years that had been wasted, or exercise the wisdom which had been acquired.

Sarah, as Disraeli's confidante, was obviously very sympathetic towards his predicament at all stages of his career (especially as she often heard only his own glowing accounts of his affairs), and what we have here may well be a typically sympathetic rendering of her brother's own self-justification. Life, in retrospect, is seen to have had a conscious form; if youth is 'wasted', it is due to an 'erroneous' *theory*, rather than to any less planned reason.

Once the actual election is under way Disraeli himself is in control of any interpretation and projection of ambition. Where Disraeli, as we have seen, felt inclined to justify his ancestors, and where he was suffering under burdensome debts, Aubrey Bohun's main qualifications for leading a new National Party are his 'high lineage' and his 'splendid fortune'. On the basis of this it is not surprising that he gets elected, and quickly becomes one of the greatest speakers in the House of Commons.

However, one should not make too much of the similarities or dissimilarities (or, indeed, ironic predictions). The work contains many other familiar Disraelian traits, and many of the most memorable passages are those which reflect the liveliness which often colours his fiction. Modern apologists sometimes ignore this in an effort to construct theories of coherence and artistic integrity in his works. The fact remains that Disraeli's writings were often slipshod, but that does not detract from the way they convey the exuberance which Disraeli obviously felt when he penned much of his fiction. The election scenes of *Hartlebury* show this as well as any of his recognised works, and when, for example, one of the partisan locals says to one of his rivals that he will 'bung up his spectacles' (carefully avoiding words like 'punch' and 'face'), we can see how much Disraeli's eye and ear were on the infinite variety of life, as much as his mind was on political theory.

Although Disraeli's meeting with Peel in 1832 appears to us, with hindsight, as an intriguing milestone in the novelist's emerging political career, a meeting which had more immediate political relevance took place at a dinner party given by Henrietta on 10 July 1834. It was there that Disraeli met Lord Lyndhurst. If Lyndhurst was not unique in terms of the political influence he had, he was at least the first prominent man of affairs to regard Disraeli as a friend. Even the fact that Lyndhurst was regarded by much of society as less than discreet was an advantage rather than otherwise as far as Disraeli was concerned. The author found himself at once the willing recipient of the highest political and social gossip. Whereas the political workings of the election in *Hartlebury* had been experienced and expressed from ground level, Disraeli was now afforded a window through which to view the social machinations which determined parliamentary and ministerial fortune. If Lyndhurst's underplayed political acumen prevented him from being a Marquess of Carabas, Disraeli was nevertheless able to fancy himself in a position which would not have been unfamiliar to Vivian Grey.

It was in the form of an open letter to Lord Lyndhurst that the novelist wrote during 1835 what Robert Blake has described as Disraeli's 'first serious contribution to political literature'.[10] December of that year saw the publication of 'A Vindication of the English Constitution in a Letter to a Noble and Learned Lord by Disraeli, the Younger'. A great deal of the *Vindication* is fanciful and eccentric, but, from the point of view of Disraeli as a novelist, it is a fascinating text when seen alongside *Coningsby* and *Sybil*. Under the guise of what often seems to be a kind of pseudo-logic, Disraeli explores lucidly the notions of English history and politics which have since become inseparably linked with his name. The fact that he never again repeated an attempt at a serious political treatise of this kind is worthy of note. When the time came for him to express the Young England ideals in the years 1841 to 1847, he was to have immediate recourse to his talents as a novelist, and it is interesting to speculate as to whether Disraeli himself acknowledged that such political ideals, mixed, as they were, with elements of absurdity, were best expressed in a medium which was unashamedly fictional in content.

During the 1830s, however, Disraeli's main concern remained the practical problem of gaining a seat in the House of Commons. Until such problems of tangible advancement were solved, and until he had attained a reasonably secure position *within* the accepted political machine, there would have been little time or purpose for combining the theories of the *Vindication* with a romantic story. As we shall see, *Coningsby* and *Sybil* emerged from a mixture of motives, only one of which was the desire to publicise a constitutional doctrine.

When Disraeli again took up his pen to write fiction, in 1836, his aim, for the first time really since the composition of *The Young Duke*, was solely a financial one. He still had the half-finished manuscript of the love story which he had begun in 1833, and as the summer of 1836 approached he started to look for a buyer for a completed version of the novel. On 13 June he wrote to his sister Sarah: 'I have agreed to let Colburn have a novel to be published on October 1, and for a greater sum than I have yet received.'[11] This time there was no hope of a work growing out of 'lounging'; Disraeli's life was now brimming over with political activity, but as long as the dunning letters continued to arrive it became an absolute necessity that one work (or more) of fiction be quickly penned and paid for. Isaac D'Israeli saw the new project with a good deal of scepticism. As he wrote to his son: 'Will the *Fictionalist* assort with the *Politician*?' It is a great pity that no record of Disraeli's reply survives, because it may have been a characteristic and theoretic justification of the double role forced on him by circumstance.

While the father was probably in ignorance as regards Benjamin's financial predicament, the son was not only tying up his love story, but also contemplating a second novel to be written within the next six months, and another one to follow that. It seems he envisaged one large assault on the market for 'popular' novels, which would earn him altogether something in the region of three or four thousand pounds. But October passed and Disraeli had still not received any money. Colburn was holding the love story back for the Christmas trade, and it was only in December that *Henrietta Temple* was finally published.

Despite the name of the 'heroine', and even though the first half had been written three years before, the novel is hardly an account of Disraeli's own passionate affair. If the type of reinterpretation of experience and the projection of ambition that we have seen in his earlier fiction can be called 'autobiography', then there is little of that in *Henrietta Temple*. But B. R. Jerman's conclusion that Disraeli's 'maturity was complete by the end of 1836, since he no longer had the need to write autobiography'[12] is only half right. If the idea of 'auto-biography' as the exploration of individual psychological and moral experience had largely disappeared with *Contarini Fleming* and *Alroy*, the need to categorise experience within a historical tradition surfaced again in *Coningsby* and *Sybil*. The differences inherent in *Henrietta Temple* (and also *Venetia*) stem as much from the circumstances under which they were written as they do from any conscious change in Disraeli's literary ideals.

By January 1837 the second of the proposed novels was at the publisher's. This was *Venetia, or the Poet's Daughter*, an unlikely romance in which the two main characters, Plantagenet Cadurcis and Marmion Herbert, were based on Byron and Shelley respectively. From Disraeli's point of view both novels were qualified successes; *Henrietta Temple* in particular earned him more money than any novel he had written since *Vivian Grey*, and it also contributed to a new growth in his popularity. It was a novel which, after *Alroy*, seemed to incorporate most of what the average reader was looking for, and at one point Henrietta Temple herself comes close to justifying the way in which Disraeli indulged the public taste for rivers of diamonds and ortolans:

> I do not despise the talent which describes so vividly a dinner and a ball . . . As far as it goes it is very amusing, but it should be combined with higher materials. In a fine novel manners should be observed and morals should be sustained; we require thought and passion, as well as costume and the lively representation of conventional arrangements; and the thought and passion will be relieved in the novel as they are relieved in life, and the whole will be more true. (*Henrietta Temple*, VI, xii)

Although the story's ostensible subject, love, involves moral decisions on the part of the main characters, there is no sense in which moral rectitude encompasses that wider range of matters, from sexual temptation to national destiny, which was apparent in *Alroy*. The

'manners' of the society Disraeli portrays in *Henrietta Temple* (especially in the second half of the novel) regulate what there is of passionate
feeling, and where the bizarre nature of *Alroy* lay in its unfettered
extravagance, the unlikeliness of the love story is inherent in its cloying
neatness. Ferdinand Armine, Henrietta's lover, has 'not the fatal gift
of imagination'. His 'passion' is rather a display of his temper, and
there is no real sense of the lovers loving. There is even a feeling that
Disraeli is being more coy than convention would demand; on the one
occasion that Ferdinand mentions children, 'Miss Temple looked
somewhat demure, turned away her face a little, but said nothing'.

If love is the supposed 'higher material' on which the first half of the
novel is based, then certainly with the second half we feel ourselves
drifting near the worlds of Vivian Grey and the Duke of St James, as
we suddenly find ourselves in the presence of such personages as Mr
Million de Stockville and Lady Ionia Colonnade. As they chatter and
jingle their way into the novel, the story is injected with a degree of
tumbling pace which reflects not only the society it is portraying, but
also the speed at which it was written. However, the disparity in the
novel's two halves should not be overstressed; considering the break in
circumstances and composition, *Henrietta Temple* maintains a good
deal of continuity. Money is as much a link as love, and if Ferdinand's
financial problems function as a trait of individual irresponsibility and
a bar to felicity in the first half, the question of personal finance is
inflated in the later parts of the book until it engulfs and directs the
entire world of manners. In many respects *Henrietta Temple* points to
aspects which featured prominently in *The Young Duke*.

The money problems which Disraeli had had in 1831 were only more
pronounced and immediate six years later. But it is a mark of his irre-
pressible wit that the subject is dealt with in no dour manner in this
novel. Indeed, Disraeli's own debts and need of cash prompted by
necessity a literary celebration rather than a lamentation. Celebration,
however, need not exclude cynicism and plain envy. When we read the
lively remarks of the man in the sponging-house as he says to Ferdinand
'It is only poor devils nabbed for their fifties and hundreds that are
ever done up. A nob was never nabbed for the sum you are, sir, and
ever went to the wall', we are reminded that Disraeli, on the brink of a
political breakthrough, was himself in danger of being 'done up'.

As a member of Parliament Disraeli (and Ferdinand Armine, for
that matter) would have been immune to prosecution for debt. In the
early idealised parts of *Henrietta Temple* being in Parliament is seen as
the equivalent of 'doing something' – something Ferdinand is prevented from doing then by virtue of his being a Catholic. But by the second
half of the novel, Parliament is seen not only as a vocation but also as
an escape; the aptly named Catchimwhocan evades his creditors by
election. In the face of such financial cynicism, the ancient and noble

families of Disraeli's society are seen to be patronising the 'new' money men, epitomised by Mr Bond Sharpe:

> Mr. Bond Sharpe had unbounded confidence in the power of capital. Capital was his deity. He was confident that it could always produce alike genius and triumph. Mr. Bond Sharpe was right: capital is a wonderful thing, but we are scarcely aware of this fact until we are past thirty; and then, by some singular process which we will not now stop to analyze, one's capital is in general sensibly diminished. As men advance in life, all passions resolve themselves into money. Love, ambition, even poetry, end in this. (*Henrietta Temple*, VI, xiii)

It would be unfair to suggest that this tone is typical of most of *Henrietta Temple*. Such remarks, however, *do* form a relevant and engaging theme in the work, and a theme, moreover, which was of no small personal interest to Disraeli in 1837. Disraeli may have dreamt not only of fortune, but also of *a* fortune, and such speculation is a legitimate spur to literary curiosity.

The same cannot be said of *Venetia*. While there is doubtless much of psychological interest to be gleaned from Disraeli's portrayal of Byron and Shelley (particularly with regard to the latter's revolutionary stance), *Venetia* is a less than accomplished salute to the manners and ideals which helped to create the young author's imagination. Its lack of interest for the less than devoted reader lies not so much in its fanciful plot, as rather in the absence, for much of its length, of that commitment and enthusiasm which can be felt in most of Disraeli's other novels. The way towards Parliament was now the most important path to be followed, and it was to be some years before full literary commitment could be regained, and harnessed with the new career. The Byron figure of *Venetia*, Cadurcis, in one of his poems, sums up a feeling which must have been close to Disraeli's own:

> My tale is done; and if some deem it strange
> My fancy thus should droop, deign then to learn
> My tale is truth: imagination's range
> Its bounds exact may touch not: to discern
> Far stranger things than poets ever feign,
> In life's perplexing annals, is the fate
> Of those who act, and musing penetrate
> The mystery of Fortune: to whose reign
> The haughtiest brow must bend. (*Venetia*, IV, xi)

That Fortune was to be Parliament, marriage and, in many ways, the beginning of a new reign.

The year 1837 was a key one in the life of Disraeli. Events of a constitutional nature dwarfed any success he might have achieved with

Henrietta Temple or *Venetia*. On 19 June William IV died and Victoria became Queen. Lyndhurst went to Kensington Palace to pledge fealty to his new sovereign, and Disraeli, who had accompanied him, waited outside. The description that Lyndhurst gave the novelist of the proceedings inside the palace formed the basis of Disraeli's account of the accession in *Sybil*. Even then the aspiring politician must have been dreaming of an 'Allegiance to one who rules over the land that the great Macedonian could not conquer; and over a continent of which even Columbus never dreamed: to the Queen of every sea, and of nations in every zone' (*Sybil*, I, vi). In the general election which automatically followed the death of a monarch, Disraeli was elected to Parliament.

His electoral success has been told and retold in the many biographical works which have charted Disraeli's political career, and there is no need to duplicate that story here. Disraeli had without doubt entered a new phase in his life: a phase marked not only by his public life, but also by a change in his personal and private affairs. The affair with Henrietta had come to a rather ignominious end in 1836. Two years later he married Mary Anne Lewis on 28 August at St George's, Hanover Square. Mary Anne has been the subject of so many affectionate anecdotes and fables, as well as serious histories, that it would be impossible in a study of this kind to reach any real assessment of the oddly successful marriage which Disraeli and his wife enjoyed. But successful it was. It gave him the security he needed to pursue his new career with assurance. His oratorical assault on the House of Commons will be remembered by politicians and historians for ever, and, if the quest for parliamentary celebrity had begun with energy rather than with tact, the scale of Disraeli's commitment obviously supported Mary Anne's claim that 'Literature he has abandoned for politics'. Six years were to pass before Disraeli published another novel.

Notes: Chapter 4

1   Quoted by Robert Blake, *Disraeli* (London: Eyre & Spottiswoode, 1966), p. 87.
2   ibid., p. 108.
3   Daniel R. Schwarz, *Disraeli's Fiction* (London: Macmillan, 1979), p. 48.
4   ibid., p. 47.
5   John Carey, *Thackeray: Prodigal Genius* (London: Faber, 1977), p. 84.
6   Blake, pp. 94–119.
7   Quoted in ibid., p. 104.
8   loc. cit.
9   The Disraeli Project, based at the Queen's University at Kingston, Ontario, is engaged on a co-ordinated programme of publication, research, graduate and undergraduate study, focused upon the works of Benjamin Disraeli. At present the Project is preparing the Complete Letters of Disraeli for publication.

10   Blake, p. 128.
11   Quoted by B. R. Jerman, *The Young Disraeli* (Princeton, NJ: Princeton University Press, 1960), p. 271.
12   ibid., p. 279.

5

Animal Magnetism, or Unknown Tongues

William Makepeace Thackeray, the desecrator of poor little partridges, in *The Diary of Jeames de la Pluche*, has Jeames write of a particular group of persons that 'They're always writing about battleaxis and shivvlery, these young chaps'. The young chaps he was referring to were all back-bench Tory MPs. There were only a few of them, but they became known collectively as 'Young England'. Whatever the political aims and aspirations of Young England may have been, and whatever parliamentary success was enjoyed by the chaps who comprised the group, it will always be associated with the pages of two works of fiction which were written in 1844 and 1845. After several years of committed political activity, during which time his pen was never engaged on any work of fiction, it was the idealised sentiment of Young England which gave Disraeli's next two novels much of their particular flavour. In *Coningsby* and in *Sybil* Disraeli the novelist, by his deftness as an artist, and by his habitual attempts to order and rationalise disparate ideals, lent grace and some genuine literary respectability to an amalgam of political ambitions and historical perspectives. That amalgam was already a lost cause by the time the novels had been published.

Once again, these novels invite us to question the link between Disraeli's fiction and 'reality'. As has been suggested, such questions do not in themselves necessarily cast doubt on the earnestness of Disraeli's intentions, and to question the 'seriousness', or importance to Disraeli's ambitions, of the apparent political didacticism in *Coningsby* or the social conditions described in *Sybil*, is not to accuse him of literary opportunism. These two novels have, quite justifiably, engaged the attention of more critics and adulators than any other of Disraeli's works. They warrant that attention because they are his most original contribution to Victorian literature, and not because they are, as has been argued frequently, innovative in a narrowly political or propagandist way.

In the introduction to *Literature and Politics in the Nineteenth Century*, John Lucas, in explanation of the contents of the book, says,

> it may be asked, where is Disraeli, where are the Chartist poets, where is early Swinburne? I might explain their absence on grounds of lack of space. But more importantly, it does not seem to me that the writers just mentioned...have produced important political literature. I do not regret not having had the space to include them.[1]

However one defines 'political literature', such a statement seems slightly absurd. Yet, at the same time, Lucas's remarks ring true about *Coningsby* and *Sybil* when one regards them in the light of Disraeli's other novels. The so-called Young England novels are not, for example, about the forming of cogent policies, or the administration of states. Neither are they about government. They reveal something of the way men and women stand in relationship to one another in society; but if *that* is 'political', it is also true of most good novels. They are rather concerned with national characteristics, heroic ideals, lofty principles and the acquisition of power by which those characteristics, ideals and principles might be achieved. As we have already seen, the obsession with an idealised rise to power for the purpose of 'principled' conduct was hardly something new in Disraeli's fiction, although in *Coningsby* the emphasis is shifted away from the 'hero's' *own* character and capability for action.

Disraeli's practical political growth after 1837 was only one of the several factors which contributed to the expressions in the Young England novels. In 1839 he made an attack in the House of Commons on the new Poor Law on the occasion of the presentation of the Chartist petition. The following year he was one of five MPs who opposed the harsh treatment meted out to the Chartist leaders. These were still, of course, early days for the emerging parliamentarian and, to his credit, one could not say that he was not independently minded in much of his thinking, even though he was still a supporter of Sir Robert Peel at this time. When, however, three years later, he finally picked up his pen again for another assault on the world of fiction, it was no simple matter of projecting through the pages of a novel those doctrines which he had seemed to espouse in Parliament. The views which Disraeli had already outlined in the *Vindication* do admittedly find frequent expression in *Coningsby* and *Sybil*, and, to a large extent, the eccentricities of the former tract sit more comfortably within the confines of a fictional plot and form. But the great advantage of the novel was not that it offered an accessible public platform for didacticism, but rather that it allowed Disraeli the chance to voice views which were not necessarily complementary, or which did not logically contribute to a cogent thesis. The narrator's capability is widened through the guise of 'characters'. Such an approach was, and is, vital to the success of *Coningsby* and *Sybil*, for through his interpretation of 'character' Disraeli was able to make his art more impersonal. *Coningsby* and *Sybil* awaken our sensibilities not by dogma, but by paradox and contradiction.

However much this may have been a conscious plan by Disraeli, there is no doubt that the total effect achieved owes as much to his natural idiosyncrasies and his eclectic taste, as it does to any preconceived challenge to literary expectations. Similarly, the Young England flavour of the novels cannot be tied to any well-defined philosophy. To examine and describe in any detail Young England within the limits of a study of this type would be an extravagance, and would necessarily reproduce the work and the ideas which have already been elegantly expressed by the most notable of Disraeli's biographers. But it must be kept in mind that the ideas or expectations of Young England were not always synonymous with those of Disraeli. Disraeli was approaching 40; he was a man somewhat soured by not already being in government, who was well aware of the disadvantages of being seen as a naive extremist. The other main members of Young England were much younger; George Smythe, Lord John Manners and Alexander Baillie-Cochrane (respectively Coningsby, Henry Sidney and Buckhurst in *Coningsby*). Of this group Manners wrote in his journal, 'this, then, is the germ of our party – no particular principles, but a hotch-potch . . .'.[2]

The hotch-potch was at least united on one thing. All of Young England was, by 1841–2, opposed to the progressive or liberal Conservatism that came to be associated with Peel. But beyond such an agreement to oppose the ensconced political philosophy of the day, Young England had the distinct air of being unworldly. Yet it was this unworldliness which accounted for its intense, albeit restricted, fervour. This should alert us to the fact that *Coningsby* and *Sybil* are notable for their fervent, misty, romantic and paradoxical hotch-potch. As far as political pamphleteering is concerned, they are fortunately impotent, like most works of art. But the qualities which *are* apparent ideally suited a literary imagination which constantly romanticised the banal, sought to order the chaotic and which saw an underlying heroic strain in the nature of man. It was another dream nurtured on books, and as the members of Young England sought guidance in literature and history, so it was that they hoped for a similar expression of their own ideals.

Disraeli's own view of history (reworked to justify much of his philosophy) looked back to Clarendon, while his fervent patriotism appealed to Bolingbroke for authority. Bolingbroke, writing in *A Patriot King* in 1749, firmly believed in a divine right to govern well, but he affirmed that 'A divine right to govern *ill* is an absurdity: to assert it, is blasphemy'. It was a language which appealed to the spirit as much as the mind, and it was a form of expression which sometimes carried within its appearance of analysis and prescription, a latent lack of precision. For example, he claimed:

> My aim is to fix this principle, that *limitations* on a crown ought to be carried *as far* as it is necessary to secure the liberties of a people; and that all *such limitations* may subsist, without weakening or endangering monarchy.

Within the context of *A Patriot King* such argument takes its place in a progressive expression of Bolingbroke's beliefs. In abstract, however, it is not very different from some of the heady and rhetorical passages which swell out the speeches of the leading characters in *Coningsby*.

In *A Patriot King* Bolingbroke expressed his dislike of Jacobitism, which, via the novels of Sir Walter Scott, Disraeli and his colleagues were attracted to on grounds of 'adventure', if nothing else. Bolingbroke's impatience with the Jacobites was based on their refusal to seek their ends *within* the existing constitution, and of this Disraeli, both in reality and in fiction, wholeheartedly approved. It is a facet of his mind which should perhaps temper our view of him as a revolutionary in any constitutional sense. As he said of Aubrey Bohun in *Hartlebury*:

> Mr. Bohun, with great talents, extensive experience, and a mind imbued with all the profound and comprehensive spirit of modern philosophy, was not insensible to the change which must occur in the relations between the governors and the governed. As a theoretical politician, he admitted this change, perhaps in its greatest possible extent: as a practical politician, he thought it the duty of a great statesman only to effect that quantity of change in the country whose destiny he regulated which could be achieved with deference to its existing constitution. (*Hartlebury*, II, i)

Nevertheless, in his Young England novels Disraeli goes out of his way to make a number of provocative anti-Whig and almost Jacobite points, as when in *Sybil* he proclaims the beneficence of Charles I's tax system. It is at such times that we realise that apparent inconsistencies in fiction can be excused on grounds other than those of pragmatism and expediency. It is another example of the expansive meaning that 'fiction' had for the author; Young England itself was a fiction for Disraeli, and only by viewing it as such could he have reconciled it to his more practical political designs.

The influence of Scott on Disraeli was not, however, merely one of romance and adventure. It is true that, with the exception of Bulwer's works, Disraeli did not read novels after Scott, and the Scottish tales contributed to the emerging literary ideals of the young man. But as far as seeing *Coningsby* and *Sybil* in a literary tradition is concerned, a novel of more importance was *Ivanhoe*. It was with this work that Scott broke from his Scottish novels; with *Ivanhoe* he was trying to write for a larger audience which would want to find something in the fiction with which to identify. It is a novel which discusses, therefore, the emergence of a unified nation, united by a government aware of responsibilities to all classes. The solution, idealistically achieved, lies in a mutual acknowledgement by all concerned of a common interest, and, through a typical Scott compromise, a balance is achieved as the hero learns to reconcile opposing forces. Such a reconciliation signals a better future.

If such a structure sounds familiar after reading *Coningsby* and *Sybil*, then that is not accidental. It would be misleading and over-schematised, however, to use the word *dialectic* of Disraeli's novels. His currency is rather that of paradox, and it is through this that we are made aware of the ideas of the novel. The novels are not propagandist in that they do not require any synthesis of their disparate views. Such 'tidiness' is a function of the plot and, in *Coningsby* and *Sybil*, the art form is brought together at the end of the novel in much the same way as in *The Young Duke* or *Henrietta Temple*. It is a tribute to Disraeli's handling of *this* side of his fiction that the papering over the cracks is not immediately apparent on a first reading.

But, of course, one of the great charms of Scott, and in particular *Ivanhoe*, for Disraeli, was the one referred to by Jeames: 'the battle-axis and shivvlery'. Chivalry was of central importance to the overall concept of Young England, and Disraeli's literary heritage, such as it was, through Scott, and his love of social decorum and grace, led him to indulge this aspect of his work. The book which Disraeli and his colleagues turned to for guidance on this issue was Kenelm Digby's *The Broadstone of Honour, or the True Sense and Practice of Chivalry*, which was first published in 1822. As Digby said, the work was called *The Broadstone of Honour* 'seeing that it would be a fortress like that rock upon the Rhine which appears to represent, as it were, knightly perfection, being lofty and free from the infection of a base world'. This large and comprehensive work was regarded as a manual by Young England, and when we consider that Disraeli's last but one novel, *Henrietta Temple*, had taken its motto from *Don Quixote*, it makes interesting reading to learn Digby's views on the advantages of studies in chivalry:

> In the first place, they serve their country by adorning its peculiar traditions and recollections; preserving alive in the memories of men the magnanimity and greatness of ages that are departed, and cherishing that poetry which lives in every people, until it is stifled by the various and factitious interests of a life devoted to luxury and avarice.

It was the preservation of 'peculiar traditions' which featured prominently in the national ideas of Young England, and which also came in
for a fair share of ridicule (as we have seen with Thackeray). Even
Monckton Milnes, who was something of a sympathiser with many of
Young England's aims, could not resist lampooning the ludicrous side
of the movement in his *Lines to a Judge* by 'a culprit actuated with
Young England sentiments':

> Oh! flog me at the old cart's tail,
> I surely should enjoy
> That fine old English punishment
> I witnessed when a boy!
> I should not heed the mocking crowd,
> I should not feel the pain,
> If *one* old English custom
> Could be brought back again!

This is one area where we probably *can* see a distinction between what
Young England (mainly Manners and Smythe) thought, and what
Disraeli believed. In *Coningsby* Disraeli brought the subject up over
dinner:

> 'Henry thinks,' said Lord Everingham, 'that the people are to be fed
> by dancing round a May-pole.'
> 'But will the people be more fed because they do not dance round a
> May-pole?' urged Lord Henry.
> 'Obsolete customs!' said Lord Everingham.
> 'And why should danging round a May-pole be more obsolete than
> holding a Chapter of the Garter?' asked Lord Henry.
> (*Coningsby*, III, iii.)

There is no doubt that Henry Sidney's riposte is backed by a winning
logic; but there is still the sense that Disraeli is satirising the absurdity
of Henry's ideals. The subject is viewed in a sympathetic light, but once
such a distancing is noticed, it becomes legitimate to question Disraeli's
commitment elsewhere. In the same journal in which he wrote of the
'hotch-potch' of Young England, Manners wrote: 'Could I only satisfy
myself that D'Israeli believed all that he said, I should be more happy:
his historical views are quite mine, but does he believe them?' The
answer must surely be, yes he did. But then he had also 'believed' in the
unscrupulousness of Vivian Grey, the dreams of Contarini Fleming
and the ambitions of Alroy. Belief, faith, a principle accepted as real,
when expressed through fiction need not be (*was* not in Disraeli's case,
as we have seen) synonymous with any solemn, static and defined set of
values. Fiction is the playground of imagination, and we should be
aware that *Coningsby* and *Sybil* are further expressions of Disraeli's

imagination, his infatuations, his eccentric ideas and his idiosyncratic style.

Disraeli was not the only member of Young England to turn to writing as a means of expressing the hotch-potch. Lord John Manners, in *A Plea for National Holy-Days* (published in 1843, and containing the plea for maypoles on which the incident in *Coningsby* was based), addressed himself to recreations and claimed that 'Utilitarian selfishness has wellnigh banished all such unproductive amusements from the land: has it not also banished contentment and good humour, and loyalty from thousands of English cottage homes'. The point is one which might conceivably have come from *Coningsby*. However, Manners's style, lacking Disraeli's structure, wit and genius, betrays, through its very direct earnestness, a certain naivety. When Manners approached verse he fared no better, as in *England's Trust* (1841), where he wrote,

> Each knew his place – king, peasant, peer, or priest –
> The greatest owned connexion with the least;
> From rank to rank the generous feeling ran,
> And linked society as man to man.

Perhaps it is fitting that he will probably always be remembered for his infamous couplet:

> Let wealth and commerce, laws and learning die,
> But leave us all our old Nobility.

George Smythe was also a 'poet'. In his collection of miscellanies, *Historic Fancies*, published in 1844, the poem 'The Merchants of Old England' paid tribute to Young England's adored Queen Victoria:

> She spoke of the Poor, and what they endure, in her low and thrilling
> tone,
> And offered a prayer that Trade might bear relief through the starving
> land,
> To the strong man's weakened arm, and his wan and workless hand.
> And by the power, that was her dower, might Commerce once more be
> The Helper of the Helpless, and the Saviour of the Free.

It is unfair to compare such effusions with *Coningsby* and *Sybil*. As novels they embrace so much more than could be encapsulated in any form of didactic writing.

Coningsby, or, The New Generation was published in May 1844 by Henry Colburn, on the agreement that the profits would be shared equally between author and publisher; Disraeli's share on 3,000 copies was therefore about £1,000. The novel met with immediate success and the first edition of 1,000 copies was sold within a fortnight. As Disraeli wrote in the preface to the fifth edition:

> Three considerable editions were sold in this country in three months; it was largely circulated throughout the Continent of Europe, and within a very brief period more than 50,000 copies were required in the United States of America.

The sales mirrored the quality of the book. It is an elegantly constructed work which, although unlikely to appeal to the modern reader as much as *Sybil*, will always be regarded by some critics as Disraeli's masterpiece.

The novel contains further examples of the traits which we have seen in his earlier works, but in *Coningsby* no one approach or infatuation is allowed to dominate at the expense of the others. We are kept aware of the healthy tension between fact and fiction, which was such an important part of Disraeli's life, as the novel moves between seemingly 'serious' diatribes and the realms of glittering society. It is a tension which animates the characters, as it intrigues the reader. Lucretia, for example, at the height of her scheming against Lord Monmouth, cannot concentrate on her French novel: 'Her own existence was too interesting to find any excitement in fiction.' The 'political' world, as it exists in the novel, is most obviously present in the voicing of opinions in private and domestic encounters, but *Coningsby* is not bereft of the practical side of electioneering. When we read of the election at Darlford, much of the prose has the tang of hard-earned experience which accounts for so much of the vigour of *Hartlebury*. When Disraeli writes of the nomination day of the election, his prose conveys a mixture of tedium and excitement, disapproval and enthusiasm:

> Nomination day altogether is a most unsatisfactory affair. There is little to be done, and that little mere form. The tedious hours remain; and no one can settle his mind to any thing. It is not a holiday, for every one is serious; it is not business, for no one can attend to it; it is not a contest, for there is no canvassing; nor an election, for there is no poll. It is a day of lounging without an object, and luncheons without an appetite; of hopes and fears; confidence and dejection; bravado bets and secret hedging; and about midnight, of furious suppers of grilled bones, brandy-and-water, and recklessness. (*Coningsby*, V, iv)

These practical and political thoughts exist, as usual, alongside Disraeli's sparkling society and his gastronomic hints. In *Coningsby* the chief appeal is for hot plates at dinner, and the French nation is chastised for serving meals on cold ones.

But if one were to look for a short and contained example of Disraeli at his most artistic one would probably choose the death of Lord Monmouth:

> Lord Monmouth had died suddenly at his Richmond villa, which latterly he never quitted, at a little supper; with no persons near him but those who were very amusing. He suddenly found he could not lift his glass to his lips, and being extremely polite waited a few minutes before he asked Clotilde, who was singing a very sparkling drinking song, to do him that service. When in accordance with his request she reached him, it was too late. The ladies shrieked, being very frightened: at first they were in despair, but after reflection, they evinced some intention of plundering the house. Villebecque who was absent at that moment arrived in time; and every body became orderly and broken-hearted. (*Coningsby*, IX, ii)

Monmouth is alone with two actresses whose company he has engaged to cheer him up. The atmosphere is one of 'amusement', suddenly halted by Monmouth's inability to drink just as one of the girls is singing a drinking song. The man whose great influence and power has been felt throughout the book is suddenly powerless. But even when stricken his first thought is for a superficial politeness. When he dies, the girls' thoughts move quickly from despair to plundering, and finally, with the intervention of Villebecque, they become 'orderly and broken-hearted'. The death is stylised, especially with Disraeli's tendency to use phrases like 'When in accordance with his request'; but it is also poignant, well-mannered and oddly logical. It is a hollow death which, while not denying the artistic justification of such a demise, evokes a sense of pity. It is easy to criticise Disraeli's language as gauche, but its formality is often fitting and acute in its perception.

It must be remembered, however, that those people who have always lauded the book most of all have usually been those readers of fiction who would not be discouraged by the long polemical statements of some of the novel's characters. Many of the readers of *Coningsby*, having enjoyed the novel in 1844, were still no nearer understanding what Disraeli was trying to achieve. The perplexity shown by some of the book's minor characters about what exactly the 'New Generation' was seeking to effect must have found a response in many of the contemporary readers: one gentleman in the novel talks of

> a sort of new set; new ideas and all that sort of thing. Beau tells me a good deal about it; and when I was staying with the Everinghams at Easter, they were full of it. Coningsby had just returned from his travels, and they were quite on the "qui vive". Lady Everingham is one of their set. I don't know what it is exactly; but I think we shall hear more of it.'
>
> 'A sort of Animal Magnetism, or Unknown Tongues, I take it from your description,' said his companion.

'Well, I don't know what it is,' said Mr. Melton; 'but it has got hold of all the young fellows who have just come out. Beau is a little bit himself. I had some idea of giving my mind to it; they made such a fuss about it at Everingham; but it requires a devilish deal of history I believe, and all that sort of thing.' (*Coningsby*, VIII, i)

The idea that *Coningsby* and *Sybil* require 'a devilish deal of history' to be understood has dominated much of the comment which the novels have generated. Disraeli's view of history is a fascinating subject, and Robert Blake has presented us with an accessible and informed account of how such a historical perspective stands up as a thesis.[3] But, valuable as such a study is, particularly for the political historian, Disraeli's art can only be fully understood after his books have been examined from all the relevant aspects of critical inspection. It is only when the novels are seen in the light of the entire canon that critics begin to appreciate what Disraeli was trying to do in *Coningsby*. It has been lucidly argued by Robert O'Kell, for example, that *Coningsby* is as much a psychological romance, in the tradition of *Contarini Fleming*, as it is a political manifesto.[4] The object of such study is not to establish any one water-tight explanation for the novel, but rather to prompt a recognition of *all* the facets of Disraeli's imagination, and his use of paradox in art.

Midway through *Coningsby* the narrator makes the claim that the work 'in an unpretending shape aspires to take neither an uninformed nor a partial view of the political history of the ten eventful years of the Reform struggle', and although we are aware that Disraeli himself did have very firm views on the subject, and although the statement appears at first to be blatantly disingenuous, any crude intentions the author might once have had become subsumed within the complex world of the novel. Various views of history are put into the mouths of the characters, and, even if by that fact, the characters lose their independence, the views are at least presented as somewhat detached. It has often been noticed that Coningsby himself has no strong individual character or sensibility, especially compared with Contarini Fleming or Alroy, and that his own actions play no part in his eventual success. This is true; but, again, it is not so much an argument for regarding the novel as a tract, but rather for examining what Disraeli was seeking to achieve with 'character'.

Disraeli would have had no real theory of what 'character' should be in literary terms. His characters were often, if not a projection of his own personality, then a crude compression of facets of his imagined society. (Monckton Milnes's comment on this subject, quoted in the following chapter, is probably the most perceptive contemporary criticism of this aspect of Disraeli's work.) In *Coningsby*, with the theme being ostensibly 'The New Generation', character represented very much the National Character. Coningsby's own apparent impotence, despite his deep personal qualities which are implied, parallels that of the nation. At the end of the book, optimism and faith in Coningsby and in the future of the country are one and the same thing. As John Holloway has said, 'put in its baldest terms, Disraeli's central premiss about the human situation is only that human society as a whole is like a live thing'.[5] As Disraeli winds himself in and out of the 'devilish deal of history', we are aware of a definite entity who is England, or English history, a maiden in distress who has been brought to her knees as a result of the inept governing she has had.

Although it is difficult always to know whether it is Disraeli's *own* view we are reading, there are certain passages which stand out as being central to the novel's overall concern. (Some, like Sidonia's long speech on the Jews, seem peripheral.) For example, there is this conversation between Coningsby and Sidonia. Coningsby speaks first:

> 'But tell me, what do you understand by the term national character?'
> 'A character is an assemblage of qualities; the character of England should be an assemblage of great qualities.'
> 'But we cannot deny that the English have great virtues.'
> 'The civilization of a thousand years must produce great virtues: but we are speaking of the decline of public virtue, not its existence.'
> 'In what then do you trace that decline?'
> 'In the fact that the various classes of this country are arrayed against each other.' (*Coningsby*, IV, xiii)

The fact that such a view was central to Disraeli's imagination is supported by the fact that in *Sybil* he went on to explore this aspect of national character more closely. But the interesting thing is that it is not a narrowly 'political' question – at least not in the way Disraeli deals with it. It is an extension of Scott's motive in *Ivanhoe*, and is a recognition that the national fate is as compelling a subject as is the fate of an isolated individual. The use of heady language, combined with the overtly religious suggestions, contributes to our feeling that the basic decline is one of faith, spirituality and the unquantifiable something which inspired Young England. If the ailment is not political, neither, then, can be the cure. Politics play an important part in the process, but political activity is seen only as one legitimate agency of action. Politics are not the subject of *Coningsby*, but they are prominent as being an obvious reflection of the national character. As Coningsby himself says:

> If the nation that elects the Parliament be corrupt, the elected body will resemble it. The nation that is corrupt, deserves to fall. But this only shows that there is something to be considered beyond forms of government – national character. And herein mainly should we repose our hopes. If a nation be led to aim at the good and the great,

depend upon it, whatever be its form, the government will respond to
its convictions and its sentiments. (*Coningsby*, VII, ii)

When, early in the book, the narrator claims 'There is no influence at
the same time so powerful and so singular as that of individual character', the statement is made on the understanding that individual
character will only achieve real success if it reflects in its pursuits the
aspirations of national character. To a large extent, it seemed, Disraeli
had finished with the ideal of the introverted individual turning away
from (Contarini) or against (Alroy) a wider historical destiny. The
move towards a more impersonal form of art was helped much by the
association with a movement which was 'national' in its ambitions;
paradoxically, the naivety of Young England helped form a new
maturity in Disraeli's art.

Much of Young England's philosophy may have been ethereal rather
than solid, but certainly by 1845 Disraeli had begun to oppose Peel and
the government in an open and direct manner. Young England may not
have been strong on realistic prescription, and in itself the imaginat-
ively based philosophy which characterised the group was no counter
to the prevalent liberal Conservatism of the day. But, in writing
Coningsby, Disraeli had made a gesture which, if it was as literary as it
was propagandist, was at least an attack on all sides of the political
status quo. Advancement for Disraeli *within* a Peelite administration
would now have been unacceptable, or, more likely, just impossible.
The only course of action was really to reinforce an ideological
independence by a concentration of criticism of the government.

Disraeli was living with the reputation of a libertine and an adven-
turer. His literary escapades had made him enemies in the Tory establishment, like Murray, Lockhart and Croker. The author of *Vivian
Grey* could hardly have been noted for his discretion or pursuance of
principle. What now if the author of *Coningsby* did not follow a path
which was anything other than independent? The usual road to respectability was, and had been for some time, closed to him. Gladstone was
more typical of the men who were already ahead of Disraeli in terms of
political preferment. It was not just the Eton and Oxford background
that Disraeli lacked; it was rather his own eccentric talents which had
made him a man marked by notoriety.

The influence he enjoyed over the other members of Young England
was no great comfort. They were in their twenties and in a sense they
were sowing political and literary wild oats. Disraeli, however, was
motivated by bitterness, despair and disdain, as much as he was by
hope and idealism. In March 1845 he attacked Peel in the House of
Commons, saying:

Dissolve if you please the Parliament you have betrayed and appeal to
the people who, I believe, mistrust you. For me there remains this at

least – the opportunity of expressing thus publicly my belief that a Conservative Government is an Organized Hypocrisy.[6]

The applause which echoed round the chamber came from the Tory back benches, as well as from the opposition. In April 1845 he was again in the forefront of attack:

> Let us in this House re-echo that which I believe to be the sovereign sentiment of this country; let us tell persons in high places that cunning is not caution, and that habitual perfidy is not high policy of State. On that ground we may all join. Let us bring back to this House that which it has for so long a time past been without – the legitimate influence and salutary check of a constitutional Opposition. Let us do it at once in the only way in which it can be done, by dethroning this dynasty of deception, by putting an end to the intolerable yoke of official despotism and Parliamentary imposture. (Loud cheers.)[7]

In May 1845 *Sybil* was published.

Artistic maturity had been achieved with a good deal of purpose, and if *Coningsby* avoided prescription, it was not short of passages which would raise important questions. But if the novel has a flaw from this point of view, it is perhaps that, in uncovering the moral and social shortcomings of the country, it is somewhat 'intellectual' in its approach. Such shortcomings exist as points in eloquent arguments, and the rottenness of the state is not seen effectively to disturb life as experienced in Coningsby Castle or Hellingsley. Even Manchester is seen from an unworldly and antiseptic point of view, represented by Mr G. O. A. Head. With his next novel Disraeli decided to approach the root problem from a more immediate angle. The next novel would be an *illustration* of the main problems discussed in *Coningsby*: a fully coloured and descriptive illustration of the disease which was afflicting the national character. Such a project would involve a degree of impersonality more apparent than in *Coningsby*. In many respects it meant that the work would be untypical of the author; but, partly because of that perhaps, *Sybil* is nowadays Disraeli's most widely read and appreciated novel.

The genesis of *Sybil, or, The Two Nations* is none too clear, although it seems that Disraeli began it soon after *Coningsby* was finished, for George Smythe wrote to him during the summer of 1844 saying, 'How are the two nations?'[8] The novel was written very quickly, considering Disraeli's parliamentary and other commitments, and it was published just one year after *Coningsby*. Disraeli wrote on May Day 1845 to his sister, Sarah:

> *Sybil* was finished yesterday; I thought it never would be; the printers were on my heels, and have been for the last month, but I don't think

it can be published till the middle of the month ... I have never been through such a four months, and hope never again. What with the House of Commons, which was itself quite enough for a man, and writing 600 pages, I thought sometimes my head must turn. I have never had a day until this, that I have felt, as it were, home for the holidays.[9]

There is not much evidence to suggest the way in which Disraeli approached the writing of a novel which was to depend on particular illustration as much as argument. There are some notes in the Disraeli Papers (Box 231), but they are short and follow no particular pattern. For example, on 'Class' there is the following:

Imperfect education of the 'English Gentleman' – ignorance of the economical sciences – and their power of useful activity circumscribed by their obvious unacquaintance with the wants, feelings and difficulties of the working classes – an ignorance arising out of the exclusive habits of the upper classes. The whole moral and intellectual development of the upper classes must be advanced before the condition of the working classes can be essentially improved.

The sentiment goes to the heart of what Young England, and particularly Disraeli, was trying to suggest. The 'unacquaintance with the wants, feelings and difficulties of the working classes' is something which is immediately associated with *Sybil*. But it is also the main subject of *Coningsby* in that the discussion, the lack of a common cause and the social ignorance are all at the centre of the political malaise of the earlier novel.

Other notes in the same small collection give an indication of Disraeli's attempt in *Sybil* to be pictorially specific. The notes are really no more than a list, but they are obviously tied in to Disraeli's intention. 'Hull Temperance Society – Female Branch; a committee of sick men living on poor men's labour; Torch-light Meetings; Infanticide; February 1839, The Convention; Steam Aristocracy; Trade Union Initiation; Baronet Order', etc. Most of these subjects can be traced to specific incidents in *Sybil*; for example, 'Infanticide' gets an airing in Book III, Chapter x, where we are told of the character Devilsdust, who, as a child, 'was sent out in the streets to "play", in order to be run over'.

Of course, such a comment shows a typical Disraelian irony, and a starkness which is often close to humour. But, nevertheless, such references are made in the novel with an air of documentation which, if sometimes *blasé*, was central to the way Disraeli expanded his art in the Young England novels. As far as the origin of specificity was concerned, Disraeli was less than candid in the Advertisement which prefaced the 1853 edition (and all subsequent editions until recently) of the novel:

the Writer had been tempted to some exaggeration in the scenes that
he has drawn, and the impressions he has wished to convey. He thinks
it therefore due to himself to state that the descriptions, generally, are
written from his own observation, and he believes that there is not a
trait in this work which official documents will not more than verify.

The Advertisement of the first edition of 1845 was more precise:

> He thinks it therefore due to himself to state that he believes there is
> not a trait in this work for which he has not the authority of his own
> observation, or the authentic evidence which has been received by
> Royal Commissions and Parliamentary Committees.

That Disraeli relied on the reports of parliamentary committees and
Royal Commissions (the Blue Books) for many of his details in illus-
trating *Sybil* has been acknowledged ever since the novel was published, but only fairly recently has it been shown conclusively what
exact reports he used and how he used them. Of course, the mention of
these Blue Books as sources raises two immediate points. One is that a
too conscious concern with secondary sources may blind us to the
author's use of irony and opportunity; Disraeli was writing, after all,
to create an effect through fiction, not to provide a reliable record of
industrial abuse. And secondly, that such a concern obscures our aes-
thetic appreciation of Disraeli's overall art in the novel. Both points are
valid. But the critic cannot afford to treat the valuable researches
which have been done in this field as peripheral in a discussion of
Disraeli's technique or aims. Part of the success of *Sybil* is that the
fervent appeals to a unified patriotism are balanced by the pictorial
industrial scenes. If the 'battleaxis and shivvlery' are still there in the
background, much of the foreground is now taken up with locksmiths
and miners.

Sheila M. Smith has shown how Disraeli used certain Blue Book
evidence in his portrayal of the fearsome town of Wodgate.[10] What
exaggeration there is in such a portrayal she puts down to Disraeli's
aim 'to confront his sheltered readers with a startling picture of pagans
in contemporary England'. If she is right (and there seems no reason to
argue against this view) then Disraeli was seeking to generate interest in
the reader through a stark clash of social settings, as he had done in
Coningsby through the expression of differing ideologies. In both
cases, realism and didacticism were not the prime objectives. Martin
Fido has taken Disraeli's use of Blue Book evidence even further.[11] For
example, he has identified the source of the Mowbray workers as *The
Factory System Illustrated in a Series of Letters to Lord Ashley* (1842),
by a crippled factory hand named William Dodd. Dodd is described as
'an exposed scoundrel; a man of great, if understandable, personal
bitterness; a writer appealing to evangelical prudery', and although

Disraeli used the more innocuous passages from this source, the novelist is nevertheless seen to be using the evidence of a document which was accepted at the time as being contaminated. It is another example (albeit in a 'good cause') of the novelist's wilful distortion of 'facts'. Fido shows the most influential Blue Book underlying the composition of *Sybil* to be *The First Report from the Midland Mining Commission, South Staffs* (1843). There are no less than twenty echoes or distinct quotations from the document in Book III, Chapters i–iii, and they lead Fido to conclude: 'It is clear from the clustering of the echoes and parallels that Disraeli often worked with the Blue Book open before him.'

It was a part of the novel which was noticed and misunderstood by the reviewers of the day. The reviewer in the *League* of 7 June 1845 said:

> The exposure of the oligarchy – its heartlessness, its selfishness – is much more complete than the delineation of the lower nation; in the first case, Mr. Disraeli has had the personal experience; in the second, he has been, for the most part, indebted for his information to Blue Books and Parliamentary Reports. He has been thus led to set forth exceptional cases as average results, and to represent the conditions of the manufacturing community as far more wretched and dangerous than it has ever been.

One only has to read Disraeli's fiction to realise that he was never interested in the 'average'; his writing is sometimes purposely and always naturally about the 'exceptional'. It was, however, the *League*'s point of view which prevailed on the question of Disraeli's interpretation of evidence. W. R. Greg, writing in the *Westminster Review* of September 1845, went so far as to say that

> 'Sybil' is not an improvement upon 'Coningsby'. The former novel was received with much approbation, from the apparent sympathy which it displayed with a suffering and neglected class. 'Sybil' will meet with far inferior success; its pictures only show how strongly and coarsely the author can paint, and are obviously not the result of any genuine regard for the poor and afflicted.

That Mr Greg himself might have had any understanding of, or regard for, 'the poor and afflicted' seems doubtful, however, in the light of a later statement he made. Speaking of the 'workers', he said:

> Our philanthropists conceive of them as masses suffering poverty and privation – our churchmen, as degraded wretches without the elements of religion or instruction – our declamatory writers, as terrific and picturesque brutes – and our statesmen, as wild and turbulent, but formidable Jacobins. Few, if any, imagine them as they

really are, – men in the receipt of earnings which, wisely husbanded and administered, would soon place them among the *easy* classes.

Admittedly, of Disraeli's 'workers', Gerard turns out to be an aristo-crat, and Devilsdust becomes a capitalist – but despite the author's obvious eccentricity, it is hardly possible for the reader to share W. R. Greg's viewpoint. The absurdities, as they do exist in the novel, are usually the results of Disraeli's infatuations, his desire to startle and his romantic plot. The reviewer of the *Examiner* of 17 May 1845 summed up the feelings of most of the contemporary critics on this aspect of the work when he said:

> One finds it difficult properly to sympathise with a Chartist delegate whose fathers fought at Agincourt, who brings writs of right for estates and peerages, and takes pride in his lineal descent from 'the last abbot of Marney'... Throughout *Sybil* in short, we find not a little clumsiness, unworthy, as we said just now, of so undeniably skilful a workman as Mr. Disraeli... [who] would not write less able and interesting books, for being a little more modest, and much less amazing.

Above all else it was Disraeli's being 'amazing' that engaged the atten-tion of most of the reviewers. Some recognised the vitality and genius in this. Most, however, if not antagonistic, were at least sober on this point. The reviewer in the *Spectator* of 17 May 1845 wrote, of the end of *Sybil*, that 'With power to combine every probable opportunity and incident of social life in the form of a fiction, philosophical Young England can only *imagine* two models of amalgamating the Two Nations – killing off the poor, or making them rich'. While this is markedly true, it perhaps implies too great a burden on the work under inspection. Disraeli wrote, in *Sybil*, a novel; he was not attempting to draft an answer to the question of the nation's disunity. To study the world of the novel, and the people who inhabit it, is to study the way Disraeli's imagination ordered, elaborated and presented society. In the end, such a study tells us more about Disraeli than it does about Young England.

Notes: Chapter 5

1 John Lucas (ed.), *Literature and Politics in the Nineteenth Century* (London: Methuen, 1971), p.3.
2 Quoted by Charles Whibley, *Lord John Manners and His Friends*, 2 vols (London: Blackwood, 1925), Vol. I, p. 145.
3 Robert Blake, *Disraeli* (London: Eyre & Spottiswoode, 1966), pp. 190–220.
4 Robert O'Kell, 'Disraeli's "Coningsby": Political Manifesto or Psychological Romance?', *Victorian Studies*, vol. 23, no. 1 (1979).

5   John Holloway, *The Victorian Sage* (London: Macmillan, 1953), p. 88.
6   Quoted by Blake, p. 187.
7   Quoted in ibid., p. 189.
8   Quoted by W. F. Monypenny and G. E. Buckle, *The Life of Benjamin Disraeli, Earl of Beaconsfield*, 6 vols (London: John Murray, 1910–20), Vol. II, p. 250.
9   Quoted in ibid., p. 251.
10 Sheila M. Smith, 'Willenhall and Wodgate: Disraeli's Use of Blue Book Evidence', *Review of English Studies*, n.s., vol. 13, no. 52 (1962).
11 Martin Fido, '"From His Own Observation": Sources of Working Class Passages in Disraeli's "Sybil"', *Modern Language Review*, vol 72, no. 2 (1977).

6

Inhabitants of Different Planets

When Thackeray moved from inspiring the pen of Jeames to writing a review of *Sybil* for the *Morning Chronicle* of 13 May 1845, he presented a more balanced opinion of Disraeli's contribution to Young England. Even so, he could not avoid the fact that, once again, the reader seemed to be required to have a devilish deal of history. He claimed that

> as a key to *Sybil*, booksellers should send down to their country correspondents a history of the Reformation, the Revolution, and of parties since the advent of the House of Hanover – a digest of the social political and commercial life of the Normans and Anglo-Saxons – a history of agriculture, manufactures, banking and credit – the works of Burke and Bolingbroke, which in *Sybil* are much discussed; and *then* the reader would be competent to judge this wonderful author.

Fortunately such a key is not an absolute necessity in judging Disraeli the novelist. Even beyond the subjects listed by Thackeray, Disraeli presents a picture which, in its variety, adds to our understanding of how he saw and expressed his world. Through the pages of *Sybil*, he ranges between high politics, industrial scenes, matters of religious principle, scenes of low life, views of the aristocracy, portrayals of injustice and violence and sketches of Chartism, all of which are held in close proximity by drama and romance, as much as they are by structure and political theory.

It has already been mentioned how Disraeli's 'political' passages tend to be fervent but misty. The following passage is typical of the tone which is struck in *Sybil*:

> In a parliamentary sense, that great party [the Tories] has ceased to exist; but I will believe that it still lives in the thought and sentiment and consecrated memory of the English nation. It has its origins in

great principles and in noble instincts; it sympathises with the lowly, it looks up to the Most High; it can count its heroes and its martyrs; they have met in its behalf plunder, proscription, and death. Nor when it finally yielded to the iron progress of oligarchical supremacy, was its catastrophe inglorious. Its genius was vindicated in golden sentences and with fervent arguments of impassioned logic by St. John [i.e. Bolingbroke]; and breathed in the intrepid eloquence and patriot soul of William Wyndham. Even now it is not dead, but sleepeth; and in an age of political materialism, of confused purposes and perplexed intelligence, that aspires only to wealth because it has faith in no other accomplishment, as men rifle cargoes on the verge of shipwreck, Toryism will yet rise from the tomb over which Bolingbroke shed his last tear, to bring back strength to the Crown, liberty to the Subject, and to announce that power has only one duty – to secure the social welfare of the PEOPLE. (*Sybil*, IV, xiv)

It is important that we keep firmly in mind the qualities that everywhere tinge the overtly political passages of the book; fervour, enthusiasm, faith, impracticability and, above all, vagueness. The positive and productive element of such prose is often no more than the implied antithesis of what Disraeli saw as the Whiggish tradition. Whiggism, we are told, was 'putrescent in the nostrils of the nation', and it was entirely dependent on Edmund Burke for its moral existence. Nothing else in the novel stokes Disraeli's rancour in quite the same way:

If a spirit of rapaciousness, desecrating all the humanities of life, has been the besetting sin of England for the last century and a half, since the passing of the Reform Act the altar of Mammon has blazed with triple worship. (*Sybil*, I, v)

Again it is an appeal to some politico-spiritual urge that may inhabit the backwaters of the reader's mind; he or she should, ideally, imbibe the heady texture of the prose without exercising too much judgement.

The history is distorted, but even so it offers us nothing that is intrinsically new, except to elevate Lord Shelburne tenuously to the Tory pantheon of Pitts, Bolingbrokes and Carterets. For the reader who is not interested in the relative upstaging of accepted figures of the past, Disraeli's pageant-like procession through the late seventeenth and eighteenth centuries, in the early part of *Sybil*, rarely becomes more than inconsequential. True, it provides the background for the political infidelities depicted within the novel; but Peel, for example, only assumes something akin to personality (in fact, it is a crude caricature) much later in the book, in his discussion with Hoaxem. Generally it is not so much the precise political accomplishments of the novel that intrigue us, as rather the overall air of excitement and mystery which emanates from them. For instance, in *Sybil*, the narrative excursion which deals with the 'Bedchamber Plot' is of interest not for its specific political repercussions, but because it is symptomatic of a general sense of factional uncertainty (an 'in-and-outedness') within the top strata of the society Disraeli is portraying.

The novel is not, however, solely concerned with the governing classes. *Sybil* merits attention for its scope which is larger than most of Disraeli's other works. Below the top layer of political intrigues Disraeli spreads out a world that is often starkly modern and progressive. Yet, at the same time, we are always kept aware of his paradoxical yearning for ancient values. It is partly because of this sometimes strained opposition of values that Disraeli's ideal future is often difficult to visualise. For example, despite the pseudo-revolutionary tone which is presented in certain passages, Disraeli maintains a stringent belief that many things, like property rights, are inviolable. Indeed, this is one of the subjects that is offered as an essential part of any modern world, and it is constantly in the foreground of the novel's discussions. Walter Gerard, whilst at the ruins of Marney Abbey, puts much of the blame for the poverty of the working classes on the Dissolution of the Monasteries, and the appropriation of the monastic lands by the neo-aristocracy: 'As long as the monks existed, the people, when aggrieved, had property on their side.' The sentiment is one which is ubiquitous in Gerard's line of thought ('what can we do; they have got the land, and the land governs the people'). However, for all Disraeli's insistence on this theme, it rarely becomes more than a motif, constantly interlacing the main bouts of action. In themselves such generalisations do not offer any real justification or stimulus for the later 'political' actions of Gerard and Morley, and nowhere does Disraeli present anything like a practical system of proposals for the reorganisation of property. (The Young England ideas on allotments were no more than a tinkering with the localised issues of landlords and tenants.) Thus it is that in dealing with progress and modernisation in *Sybil*, Disraeli was essentially addressing himself to the problems of the urban population.[1] In terms of urban development, the two main symptoms of the changing world for Disraeli were, not surprisingly, the railways and the factories.

Railways occur in several of his novels (an unexceptional fact considering the turbulent effect they had on nineteenth-century society), and they form an ideal symbol for modernisation and industrialisation. We recall, for example, Dickens's *Dombey and Son*, where we see the two sides of the topical coin; the railway destroys, in sweeping away Staggs's Gardens and the house of the Toodles family, and the railway creates by also employing the same Mr Toodles within its beneficent bounds. Most of Disraeli's references to these 'fiery devils'[2] are less obviously profound. In *Coningsby* we learn how the railway timetables are having their influence on idiomatic speech: 'he had to go three miles to the train, which started, as his friend of the previous night would phrase it, at 9-45.' In *Tancred* we hear how, on the one hand, the hero is aghast to find that the age of technology might be encroaching on his spiritual home ('"A railroad!" exclaimed Tancred, with a look of horror. "A railroad to Jerusalem!"'), while the more practical (if pecuniary affairs are so considered, as against those of the spirit) repercussions of the railways are brought home in a note which is delivered in connection with the defeat of Brunel's broad-gauge track: 'The Narrow Gauge has won. We are utterly done: and Snicks tells me you bought five hundred more [broad gauge shares] yesterday, at ten. Is it possible?' Mr Phoebus in *Lothair* remarks that 'one can do anything in these days of railroads', while in *Endymion* we find that the letting of Hurstley is a problem because of the lack of such a thing. Within *Sybil* such references are placed to reflect more obviously the social significance of such a technical advance, and in so doing they contribute to the overall paradoxical tone of the novel. In a conversation with Sybil ('the Religious') Stephen Morley makes it clear that for him the railroad is on the side of liberty and progress:

> 'Now, tell me, Stephen,' said the Religious, turning her head and looking round with a smile, 'think you it would not be a fairer lot to bide this night at some kind monastery, than to be hastening now to that least picturesque of all creations, a railway station.'
> 'The railways will do as much for mankind as the monasteries did,' said Stephen.
> 'Had it not been for the railway, we should never have made our visit to Marney Abbey,' said the elder of the travellers [i.e. Walter Gerard, Sybil's father]. (*Sybil*, II, viii)

This is later expanded upon in an interview with Lord Valentine when Morley says that 'Modern science has vindicated the natural equality of man', although, perhaps understandably, the aristocrats in general do not feel his enthusiasm for the railway. Lord de Mowbray says 'I feel it has a very dangerous tendency to equality', and he adds that 'Equality, Lady Marney, equality is not our "metier". If we nobles do not make a stand against the levelling spirit of the age, I am at a loss to know who will fight the battle.' Lord Marney shares the sentiment, and extends the subject to progress in general: 'Railroads are very good things, with high compensation . . . and manufactories not so bad, with high rents; but, after all, these are enterprises for the canaille, and I hate them in my heart.'

If the railway epitomised the speed with which technological progress moved, it was the scarred and blackened countryside which most obviously reflected the social stagnation which that 'progress' meant for most of the population. Take, for example, the following three passages:

The Black Country is anything but picturesque. The earth seems to have been torn inside out. Its entrails are strewn about; nearly the entire surface of the ground is covered with cinder-heaps and mounds of scoriae [cellular lava]. The coal, which has been drawn from below ground is blazing on the surface. The district is crowded with iron furnaces, puddling furnaces and coal-pit engine furnaces. By day and by night the country is glowing with fire, and the smoke of the iron-works hovers over it. There is a rumbling and clanking of iron forges and rolling mills. Workmen covered with smut, and with fierce white eyes, are seen moving about amongst the glowing iron and dull thud of forge hammers.

On every side, and as far as the eye could see into the heavy distance, tall chimneys, crowding on each other, and presenting that endless repetition of the same, dull, ugly form, which is the horror of oppressive dreams, poured out their plague of smoke, obscured the light, and made foul the melancholy air. On mounds of ashes by the wayside, sheltered only by a few rough boards, or rotten pent-house roofs, strange engines spun and writhed like tortured creatures; clanking in their iron chains, shrieking in their rapid whirl from time to time as though unendurable, and making the ground tremble with their agonies.

Notwithstanding the whole country might be compared to a vast rabbit warren, it was nevertheless intersected with canals crossing each other at various levels, and though the subterranean operations were prosecuted with so much avidity that it was not uncommon to observe whole rows of houses awry, from the shifting and hollow nature of the land, still, intermingled with heaps of mineral refuse or of metallic dross, patches of the surface might here and there be recognised, covered, as if in mockery, with grass and corn, looking very much like those gentlemen's sons that we used to read of in our youth, stolen by the chimneysweeps and giving some intimations of their breeding beneath their grimy livery. But a tree or a shrub – such an existence was unknown in this dingy rather than dreary region.

These three passages were written by such diverse persons as James Nasmyth, one of the most eminent mechanical engineers of the nineteenth century, Charles Dickens and Benjamin Disraeli respectively.[3] They have their obvious differences and qualities, but they share a similarity of concern. Such wholesale and panoramic description of the Victorian industrial scene was fairly common in nineteenth-century literature (or documentation, as in Nasmyth's case), and Disraeli was not alone, or even particularly individual, in his intention. Where, however, Nasmyth's account was based wholly on what he saw, and where Dickens shows us evidence of the way the author's imagination was lit up by an apocalyptic view of machines, Disraeli's passage, as has been shown by Martin Fido, is lifted from *The First Report from the Midland Mining Commissioners, South Staffs* (1843), and based on the words of the aptly named commissioner Thomas Tancred. Throughout Disraeli interprets his sources and brings them into the realm of his own novel by an injection of his familiar irony and the use of his often odd-sounding and ponderously archaic language (the passage just quoted contains a sentence of over a hundred words). Here is another example:

> The plain is covered with the swarming multitude: bands of stalwart men, broadchested and muscular, wet with toil, and black as the children of the tropics; troops of youth – alas! of both sexes, – though neither their raiment nor their language indicates the difference; all are clad in male attire; and oaths that men might shudder at, issue from lips born to breathe words of sweetness. Yet these are to be – some are – the mothers of England! But can we wonder at the hideous coarseness of their language when we remember the savage rudeness of their lives? Naked to the waist, an iron chain fastened to a belt of leather runs between their legs clad in canvas trousers, while on hands and feet an English girl, for twelve, sometimes for sixteen hours a-day, hauls and hurries tubs of coal up subterranean roads, dark, precipitous, and plashy: circumstances that seem to have escaped the notice of the Society for the Abolition of Negro Slavery. (*Sybil*, III, i)

The picture painted is, of course, one of shameful exploitation; yet somehow such descriptions, despite their authenticity, never fully convince us of their reality. In this passage, for all Disraeli's efforts at evoking the unfortunate women (with details of the 'leather', 'chain' and 'canvas'), we never actually *see* them, as we see, for example, Dandy Mick or Chaffing Jack, and too often we find ourselves ignoring the 'swarming multitude'. In contrast, the success of, say, *Mary Barton* as a social novel is due more to the gradual agglomeration of particulars than it is to any sweeping portrayal of 'the Victorian scene'.

Thus it is that the success of Disraeli's picture of industrial society is often reliant on such particulars. For example, in Book I Chapter xiii we have the old man who 'muffled up in a thick coat, and bearing in his hand what would seem at first glance to be a shepherd's crook', wakes the factory girls with a 'rattling noise' on the window panes. Again the passage has its origin in a Blue Book; this time the description comes from William Dodd, who described the old man's instrument as 'made for the purpose of making a great noise on the glass windows without breaking them, and . . . somewhat similar to a shepherd's crook, only longer in the handle, to enable the person using it to reach the upper windows'. Even though the picture is not Disraeli's own, at least here the transference seems to have contained some artistic merit. We are at first interested in the old man's job – it is an intriguing comment on the type of organisation this society demands. Only then are we struck by the fact that what he is carrying looks like a shepherd's crook. Through the use of the admittedly corrupt Dodd letters, the displacement of the rural population into the town is subtly evoked, and then rendered poignant by our realisation that this old man, even now, has a flock of sorts to attend. In comparison with such particulars, Warner's soliloquy on 'labour' (the source of which has not been identified) in the same chapter, seems uninteresting and unnecessarily didactic.

When it comes to the factories themselves, Disraeli is capable of presenting a graphic description of efficiency:

> a single room, spreading over nearly two acres, and holding more than two thousand work-people. The roof of groined arches, lighted by ventilating domes at the height of eighteen feet, was supported by hollow cast-iron columns, through which the drainage of the roof was effected. The height of the ordinary rooms in which the work-people in manufactories are engaged is not more than from nine to eleven feet; and these are built in stories, the heat and effluvia of the lower rooms communicated to those above, and the difficulty of ventilation insurmountable. At Mr. Trafford's, by an ingenious process, not unlike that which is practised in the House of Commons, the ventilation was also carried on from below, so that the whole building was kept at a steady temperature, and little susceptible to atmospheric influence. (*Sybil*, III, viii)

In Mr Trafford we have the obvious signs of a 'good' industrialist, and later Disraeli puts into the mouth of one of the agitators an ironical comment which demonstrates the factory owner's style of policy: '''He is a most inveterate capitalist,'' said Field, ''and would divert the minds of the people . . . by allotting them gardens and giving them baths.'''

Trafford, however, is the exception. Elsewhere the industrial references in *Sybil* contribute more usually to an overall impression of malpractice. For example, there is the firm of 'Shuffle and Screw' which employs bate-tickets (notes informing recipients of deductions in money wages) and fines in order to avoid paying its workers. And there are many other symptoms of a society in decline which pertain directly to these practices; the break-up of the Warner family is caused by the preference shown by employers for cheaper youth labour. In many ways the most memorable travesty is the 'Tommy' shop[4] run by Diggs and his son, Master Joseph. The son, an 'infuriated little tyrant', impresses himself easily on a mind susceptible to Dickensian grotesqueness:

> You tall gal, what's your name, you keep back there, or I'll fetch you such a cut as'll keep you at home till next reckoning. Cuss you, you old fool, do you think I am to be kept all day while you are mumbling here? Who's pushing on there? I see you, Mrs. Page. Won't there be a black mark against you? Oh! it's Mrs. Prance, is it? Father, put down Mrs. Prance for a peck of flour. I'll have order here. You think the last bacon a little too fat: oh! you do, ma'am, do you? I'll take

care you shan't complain in futur; I likes to please my customers.
(*Sybil*, III, iii)

Master Joseph, 'a short, ill favoured cur, with a spirit of vulgar oppres-
sion and malicious mischief stamped on his visage', dominates the
scene, dealing out his rough justice (Disraeli uses the word 'reckoning'
advisedly) and parodying the biblical parable,

> 'I was first, Master Joseph,' said a woman, eagerly...
> 'If you were first, you shall be helped last,' said Master Joseph, 'to
> reward you for your pains.'

The fact that Disraeli chose to portray the worst of the corruption at
the almost nightmarish town of Wodgate (rather than at, for example,
Mowbray) may be indicative of the untypical nature of some of the
happenings there. But if not exactly typical, the evils of Wodgate do, as
Sheila M. Smith has shown, have their origin in fact. He exaggerates,
for example, the Godlessness of Wodgate; Willenhall (a small town
near Wolverhampton), on which it was based, was never quite as
heathen as Disraeli would have us believe. At the same time his ideas of
modesty made him leave out some of the seamier details of the dung,
dirt-heaps and excreta in the town. He overemphasised the lack of
learning (in reality Willenhall *did* have a school), the lack of cleanliness
and the lack of redress that an apprentice would have had for wrongs
committed against him; an isolated case in a Blue Book ('An apprentice has been struck down insensible by a blow from the ironhead of a
hammer') becomes in *Sybil* an accepted rule (the masters, it seems, are
'in the *habit* of felling them with hammers...'). The enduring power
of Disraeli's coverage of this industrial scene, however, lies in more
than just this documentation, or pseudo-documentation. It is his
pungent tone of irony that allows Disraeli to avoid the pitfalls of
sentimentality without sacrificing his humanitarian stance; at their
worst his 'socially aware' passages are flat, unconvincing and counter-
productive, but at their best they are ironic, crisp and justly disturbing.

Much of the significance of the Wodgate scenes lies in the comparison that Disraeli makes between the 'Wodgate Aristocrats' (like the
so-called 'Bishop') and the real aristocrats, regarding the acceptance of
the responsibility which goes with the privileges of their respective
positions. The greatest denial of responsibility, however, involves the
church. In *Sybil* the church is seen as a potentially great social and
spiritual organ. Disraeli's references blur many of the distinctions
between Anglicanism and Roman Catholicism; it is with Catholicism
that the monastic lands and Sybil herself are so closely tied, and the
author often sounds a note akin to that of popish adulation. Young
England, after all, had had close ties with the Oxford movement; they

were both romantic movements when Romanticism was reactionary rather than revolutionary. As Joseph E. Baker has said:

> the early Oxford Movement was largely the religious side of a movement that was Tory on its social side. I should hesitate to call either a cause of the other, in any fundamental sense. Of course, there was a close interaction between these two branches of reaction, but they were both manifestations of the same spirit, already found together in Scott.[5]

Disraeli was well aware of which way the wind was blowing, and he realised the political dangers of a close literary association with Puseyism. Sybil's Catholicism is, therefore, a faith of tradition and paternalism; it never becomes a theological dogma. In fact, in *Lothair* Disraeli was to attack an invidious Roman Catholicism which, with its gaudy trappings and pomp, represented for him little more than the traditional 'scarlet lady'.

As the plot of *Sybil* evolves we are made more and more aware of Disraeli's view that the church has abandoned its responsibility towards society. He is at pains, for example, to stress the heathen nature of Wodgate (beyond, as has been noted, what was strictly factual): 'Wodgate, or Wogate, as it was called on the map, was a district that in old days had been consecrated to Woden, and which appeared destined through successive ages to retain its heathen character.' The town even has a self-appointed secular 'bishop'; as the character Tummas tells Morley, 'it has always been so that Wodgate has been governed by a bishop; because as we have no church, we will have as good'. Add to that the fact that the Chartists meet at the 'Druids Altar', and it is easy to see why Mr St Lys, the vicar of Mowbray, thinks as he does: 'I blame only the Church. The church deserted the people; and from that moment the church has been in danger and the people degraded.' Walter Gerard translates the sentiment into the wish of an activist: 'if we could only have the Church on our side, as in the good old days, we would soon put an end to the demon tyranny of Capital'. Although Disraeli never sanctions anything akin to militancy himself, he does share the wish for a combination of forces including the church. Such an alliance would clearly solve many of his problems, and when Egremont makes a gift of a volume of Thomas à Kempis to Sybil, and later when they meet in Westminster Abbey, we feel that we are being presented with tokens of an impending solemn marriage between the aristocracy and the church – a union which, Disraeli pleads, will be in the interests of the working classes.

In *Sybil*, then, we have a world trying to reconcile modern expectations with ancient values, rampant industrialisation and a church that has abdicated its responsibilities. The result, it is implied, is social division. The one great catch-phrase that *Sybil* has handed down to us is 'The Two Nations', and to examine the seemingly irreconcilable sides of Disraeli's world would appear to be to penetrate the heart of the novel. It is therefore worth quoting here the famous passage to which every commentator refers (the elder stranger is Gerard; the younger is Morley):

> 'This is a new reign,' said Egremont, 'perhaps it is a new era.'
> 'I think so,' said the younger stranger.
> 'I hope so,' said the elder one.
> 'Well, society may be in its infancy,' said Egremont slightly smiling; 'but, say what you like, our Queen reigns over the greatest nation that ever existed.'
> 'Which nation?' asked the younger stranger, 'for she reigns over two.'
> The stranger paused; Egremont was silent, but looked inquiringly.
> 'Yes,' resumed the younger stranger after a moment's interval. 'Two nations; between whom there is no intercourse and no sympathy; who are as ignorant of each other's habits, thoughts, and feelings, as if they were dwellers in different zones, or inhabitants of different planets; who are formed by a different breeding, are fed by a different food, are ordered by different manners, and are not governed by the same laws.'
> 'You speak of —' said Egremont, hesitatingly.
> 'THE RICH AND THE POOR.' (*Sybil*, II, v)

Much has been said about, and many conclusions drawn from, this passage. Patrick Brantlinger, for example, went right to the heart of the matter when he pointed out that 'Disraeli treats the two nations theme as a paradox that he hopes will startle his readers into some awareness of the problems of the poor, but he also treats it as a dangerous illusion and a cliché of radicals like Morley'.[6] Disraeli does undoubtedly show us in *Sybil* scenes of rich life and scenes of poor life, but it would be a mistake to think that he wanted the distinctions swept away completely. Once again his precise notions are (often intentionally) foggy and romantic, and we do best to sidestep the apparent issue of class-conflict. This is not necessarily to dodge the main question, for we must remember that *Sybil* is a novel, not a political tract, and there is a danger that the oft-quoted passage above, especially when presented out of context, oversimplifies the matter. If we look at the related theme of aristocracy and democracy, we get much closer to what Disraeli was saying, and we see that his concern (as an essentially romantic novelist) was as much for interesting characters and perennial truths as it was for social dichotomies.

The aristocracy of *Sybil* is not a particularly noble institution, founded, as we are repeatedly informed, on the wealth accruing from the Dissolution of the Monasteries, and the revolution of 1688. It is a class of otherwise dubious origin, nurtured on the resignation of responsibility and the factious craving for preferment, sweltering in indolence. The atmosphere is clearly established in the opening pages of the novel, when the 'vast and golden saloon' of a London club is compared, not unfavourably, with the Versailles of pre-revolution France. The place is full of 'persons consuming with a heedless air, delicacies for which they had no appetite', who indulge in drinks which are 'incomprehensible mixtures bearing aristocratic names', and who enjoy quaffing bad wine because 'one gets so bored with good wine'. Lord Eugene de Vere and Alfred Mountchesney are typical of this class, for both 'had exhausted life in their teens, and all that remained for them was to mourn, amid the ruins of their reminiscences, over the extinction of excitement'. A simple application of the 'RICH' and 'POOR' argument would condemn these dandies as irresponsible toffs who would be better off under the blade of a guillotine. The truth is, however, that Disraeli the novelist found them, and their affectations, oddly attractive.

If he were always writing about class-conflict even Disraeli would find it difficult to justify the existence and ultimate well-being of some of his characters. As it is, the only *overt* argument in favour of the aristocracy not to come from Egremont, is put into the mouth of Lord Valentine, who receives the petitioners, Gerard and Morley, in his apartment. Again, as with much of Disraeli's thought on church affairs, we are forced to accept the author's own terms, and when Valentine says simply 'You are democrats. I am an aristocrat' it seems pointless to murmur any discontent about oversimplification. The 'Two Nations' issue, however, becomes increasingly less simple as we find ourselves making references to what we know of Disraeli's view of paternalistic Toryism in order to back up what Valentine is saying. His message is that, for good or for ill, mankind is divided into classes, each one with its duties and responsibilities, and each one with its privileges and expectations. However, what often seems sustained optimism on the part of the author (as regards the better society we can expect *within* this class structure, if only people would recognise their duties) is only really encouraged in the action of the novel by the deeds of one man – Egremont. The fact that the ideas of one man can be presented at the end of the novel as something akin to a salvationary force is not so much a tribute to Disraeli's political philosophy as it is to his deftness as a novelist. This impression becomes even clearer when we realise that those key characters, who we had been led to believe were upright workers, are in reality aristocrats. The reader could be forgiven for thinking that nothing has been solved at the end of the novel. Take, for example, the factory-owning Trafford family. Baptist Hatton's sympathy for them ('I am sorry for the Traffords; they have old blood in their veins') is based not on professional esteem, moral character, or on their merits as reforming industrialists, so much as on the vintage of their red corpuscles. Disraeli has been called a Tory democrat, but there is not much of the democrat here.

But what, after all, do we see of Disraeli's democracy? It is sometimes a mixture of principles and practicalities, combining the urge for material gain with a certain amount of political intent; for example, we have the bookmaker, Hump Chippendale, who was 'a democratic leg, who loved to fleece a noble, and thought all men were born equal – a consoling creed that was a hedge for his hump'. Is there not a cruel bitterness in Disraeli's tone here that gets below the mere political questions to a deeper truth about the world and human character? Again, with Dandy Mick, we have a prospective trade unionist and a stolid supporter of Chartism who can say that his Julia told him 'she would go to the cannon's mouth for the Five Points any summer day'. Nevertheless, Dandy Mick (who is, as it turns out, also a prospective capitalist), and presumably Disraeli himself, does not feel that such a political end is incongruous with class distinctions. In fairness to Mick's ambivalence, the historical *six* points[7] were constitutional measures that did not involve the wholesale butchery of the toffs. Even so, Mick's less than courteous treatment of the waiter in Chaffing Jack's 'Temple' seems a little wanting in terms of worker solidarity. In a similar way the authorial Disraeli himself looks down on Lord Mowbray because the peer is descended from a waiter: 'His lordship was apt to be too civil. The breed would come out sometimes. To-day he was quite the coffee-house waiter.' It would be tempting to say that this is not so; to say that Disraeli is only looking down on Mowbray because the lord is not willing to *acknowledge* his genuine lineage. If Lord Mowbray were indeed only being accused of snobbishness, this explanation would be acceptable. The fact is, however, that we can never really convince ourselves that Disraeli is not smirking at him because he is low-class. The fact that the worker Mick escapes such authorial condescension is partly due to his verve and his social position, and partly because he has endeared himself as a character so much to his creator that he can avoid persecution with impunity. Again, it is Disraeli's sleight of hand; we never see the worker at work, and he is left mainly unscathed by the working-class agitation of the novel – Chartism.

Important as Chartism is as a backcloth for *Sybil*, we would be disappointed if we expected Disraeli to deal specifically with this topic.[8] For one thing, Disraeli was not trying to write a novel about Chartism in particular; and he would not, in 1845, have been able to write objectively about it if he had wanted to. If Disraeli's intentions in this respect can be reduced to simple terms, it could be said that the reasons for the inclusion of the descriptions of Chartist rioting are twofold; first, he wished to demonstrate that riotous behaviour benefits no one, not even the working classes; and secondly, he wanted to show that, fundamentally, the agitators were not principled men, like Gerard, but thugs, like the Bishop. If we accept this as Disraeli's rudimentary principle in his delineation of Chartism, there seems little to be gained from asking 'Is the author's picture of Chartism accurate?' and 'What were his views concerning the six points?'

As has already been mentioned, Disraeli was, in 1840, one of the five MPs who opposed the harsh treatment given to some of the Chartist leaders, but, in reading *Sybil*, we must keep a mindful distinction between the politician and the novelist. Once again we see the novelist more interested in the human response to the political activity than he is in the political activity itself. Devilsdust says that Stephen Morley 'knows the principles of society by heart. But Gerard gets hold of the passions', and *Sybil* can broadly be seen as an attack on both attitudes in their respective extremes. Morley's intervention, in political terms, is seen as anomalous, because it was the very failure of the Owenite industrial experiments which helped to contribute to the agitation; and Gerard's 'passion', despite its often obvious moderation, is too much the latent power of riot.

In fact, as the novel progresses Disraeli equates Chartism with anarchism, and we are left in no doubt concerning the immediate causes of the uprisings: 'no one could have imagined that the Bishop or any of his subjects had ever even heard of the Charter, much less that they could by any circumstances comprehend its nature, or by any means be induced to believe that its operation would further their interests or redress their grievances'. The picture is then made completely bathetic by Disraeli's ironic comment that the march from Wodgate 'was perhaps the most striking popular movement since the Pilgrimage of Grace'. The one beneficent act achieved by the mob is the siege of Diggs's 'Tommy' shop, and even this, though exercising a sort of reciprocal rough justice, hardly raises the quality of life in the long term for the inmates of Wodgate. It is significant, however, that in dealing with Chartism, Disraeli's imagination was most fired by the apocalyptic side of affairs: 'The music and the banners denoted the arrival of the leaders of the people. They mounted the craggy ascent that led to the summit of the Druid's Altar, and there, surrounded by his companions, amid the enthusiastic shouts of the multitude, Walter Gerard came forth to address a TORCH-LIGHT MEETING.'

As we have already noticed, the religious (or irreligious) connotations of this, and of the 'Monster Meeting of the Moor', are not accidental. Even so, such spectacles are seen as basically impulsive and transitory; if they are to mean anything at all, the impression must be sustained on those in positions of power. It is shown that the Chartists themselves think little of party politics:

To the Chartists indeed the factious embroilment at first was of no great moment, except as the breaking up and formation of cabinets might delay the presentation of the National Petition. They had long ceased to distinguish between the two parties who then and now contend for power. And they were right. Between the noble lord who goes out and the right honourable gentleman who comes in, where is the distinctive principle? (*Sybil*, IV, xv)

Disraeli does not himself, of course, waver from his own beliefs in constitutional processes and parliamentary democracy, although he is more than willing to admit the faults that lay entrenched in his adopted social class. In fact, the scenes in the novel which deal with the reception of Chartist news in 'high' places are in many ways more symptomatic of the social blindness of the 'Nation(s)' than are the impetuous gatherings of the 'People'. Mr Berners is, unfortunately, typical:

'Terrible news from Birmingham,' said Mr. Egerton at Brookes'. 'They have massacred the police, beat off the military, and sacked the town. News just arrived.'
'I have known it these two hours,' said a grey-headed gentleman, speaking without taking his eyes off the newspaper. 'There is a cabinet sitting now.'
'Well I always said so,' said Mr. Egerton; 'our fellows ought to have put down that Convention.'
'It is deuced lucky,' said Mr. Berners, 'that the Bedchamber business is over, and we are all right. This affair in the midst of the Jamaica hitch would have been fatal to us.' (*Sybil*, V, i)

Even here, however, although the satire may be aimed at Berners's treatment of the political manoeuvring as a party game, the whole spirit of the novel forces us to accept such self-centred irresponsibility as one of the facets of political life. The one thing that remains clear is that the Chartist movement can do nothing to change human nature.

Against this background of society, Disraeli portrays a wide range of characters; wider, in fact, than is to be found in any other novel he wrote. The two extremes are, of course, the aristocrats and the workers, and at both ends of the scale we find the sharply drawn caricatures which we come to expect from the author. But before pointing to their several characteristics, it is perhaps best to consult the words of one of Disraeli's contemporaries, Monckton Milnes, on the subject.[9] He deals particularly with the fact that so many of Disraeli's sketched personalities are drawn from living persons, and, what is more, intended to be known by the reader as such:

for, the moment a character is known to represent Lord – – or Mr. – –, it loses all power as a work of art. The 'historical picture' becomes the 'portrait of a gentleman'; the fidelity of the likeness is the only object of attention, not the moral fitness, the entireness, the beauty or the grandeur of the character. The great poet or novelist should mould his men and women out of the large masses of humanity, out of the manifold variety of strivers and losers, and actors and sufferers; and surely he degrades his function when he condescends to draw miniatures of individuals composing the least distinctive and frequently most vapid of all classes of the community – namely that which is conventionally called the highest.[10]

This is less true of *Sybil* than it is of, say, *Vivian Grey* or *Coningsby*, but it is in general indicative of Disraeli's failure to create individual characters in their own right. Even though in his Young England novels Disraeli was concerned with *national* character, Milnes's comments are still a valid criticism of the writer as an artist.

Of the workers in *Sybil*, Widow Carey comes alive for us at her Mowbray meat stall, and her speech (often, as with many of the 'lower' characters, a hotch-potch dialect) is one way that Disraeli makes his comments on the industrial malpractices: '"Soul alive, but those Shuffle and Screw are rotten, snickey, bad yarns," said Mistress Carey. "Now ma'am, if you please; fi'pence ha'penny; no, ma'am, we've no weal left. Weal, indeed! you look very like a soul as feeds on weal."' Her ensuing exchange with Dandy Mick Radley, when she accuses him of giving her some of his 'imperence', in similarly 'picturesque'. But such figures never really fulfil even their potential as caricatures, and so they never endear themselves to the reader as many of Dickens's absurd characters do. Despite the feeling one has of a large population in the novel, one remains mostly indifferent to the actions and fates of many of the personages. Nowadays, admittedly, our response to Victorian incarnations of 'good' and 'evil' have changed; we read *The Old Curiosity Shop* for Quilp and find Little Nell's death over-sentimental. A novelist of Dickens's calibre, however, can always evince some kind of positive reaction. In *Sybil* we find that Gerard's fate is as uninteresting and seemingly inconsequential as Lord Marney's. Of course, it might be argued that this is because Disraeli's characters have finally to submit to an authorial theme. If that is so, it is a reason but not an excuse.

In fact, on occasions, the natural characteristics of Disraeli's figures seem to be at variance with what would seem to be one of the general intentions of the book. Take, for example, the sentence about Devilsdust referred to in the previous chapter: a poor abandoned waif, 'sent out in the street to "play", in order to be run over', he survives, living off the garbage and sleeping among dungheaps, cesspools and rotting corpses, until he finally becomes a stolid worker. As a sullen prole he gives vent to such remarks as 'We shall never get our rights till we leave off consuming exciseable articles', and 'Labour may be weak, but Capital is weaker . . . Their capital is all paper.' And then, after all this, he ends up as a successful capitalist (now called Mr Mowbray) in his own business with Mick Radley. Now, presumably Disraeli wishes us to share his apparent authorial abhorrence at the conditions in which Devilsdust grew up; but, as the novel progresses and we see what a level-headed lad he is growing up to be, we seem to find ourselves presented not with an argument for improving the circumstances of such children's upbringing, but for *not* improving them.

It is as if some divine authorial hand is moving the character along from proletarian agitation to comfortable capitalism without allowing him to fulfil his *own* destiny. Again – this time at the other end of the social scale – with Lord Marney, we are told that 'He had formed his mind by Helvetius, whose system he deemed irrefutable, and in whom alone he had faith'. But despite reminders of his 'Puck-like malignity', we have to take his apparent sceptical, materialist and hedonist character very much on trust. Admittedly we hear him declaim against 'high' wages, and we see him bullying his wife; but he is never really developed as the terrible man and landlord he is supposed to be.

What is it that distinguishes Walter Gerard? Egremont reflects Disraeli's thoughts in saying that Gerard is the only trustworthy rebel in a basically bad bunch; but Gerard also exists – in a diminutive way – as a tragic figure, in that he has something akin to the old-fashioned 'fatal flaw'. The fact that we cannot sympathise with him to any great extent is due to our feeling that this 'flaw' has been too obviously fostered on him by the author. Gerard is an orator: 'I never could express my ideas except with my tongue; and there I feel tolerably at home.' This in itself would not require comment, were it not for the fact that it is crudified by Disraeli's persistent comparison between Gerard, the man of the spoken word, and Morley, the man of the written word. As it is, the Gerard of the early part of the novel is too 'sensible'; he is shown as a time-honoured foreman at Trafford's factory, with his own cottage, two pounds a week in wages, a devoted daughter and a vein of philosophical conversation that suggests resolution coupled with patience. His movement towards conspiracy, intrigue and treason (necessary if Disraeli is to justify his death in the ultimate common interest) is, therefore, not wholly convincing. Even so, Gerard's remarks still form a major part of Disraeli's overall presentation of the 'political' situation. For example, having left his imprisonment, he says of Stephen Morley: 'He still preaches moral force, and believes that we shall all end in living in communities. But as the only community of which I have personal experience is a gaol, I am not much more inclined to his theory than heretofore.'

Stephen Morley, in fact, is a figure of considerable interest, not as a character, but as a type. His makes his ideological standpoint clear as soon as we meet him: 'There is no community in England; there is aggregation, but aggregation under circumstances which make it rather a dissociating than a uniting principle.' This is said at the ruins of Marney Abbey where Morley expands on his idea in his characteristic idiom which never deviates into common banter or chit-chat: 'It is a community of purpose that constitutes society . . . without that, men may be drawn into contiguity, but they still continue virtually isolated.' On one level the novel insists that it is the breaking up of the family (for example, the Warners) that is responsible for much of the misery. Morley sees this type of social disintegration as a positive merit:

> You lament the expiring idea of home. It would not be expiring, if it were worth retaining. The domestic principle has fulfilled its purpose. The irresistible law of progress demands that another should be developed. It will come; you may advance or retard, but you cannot prevent it. It will work out like the development of organic nature. In the present state of civilization and with the scientific means of happiness at our command, the notion of home should be obsolete. Home is a barbarous idea; the method of a rude age; home is isolation; therefore anti-social. What we want is community. (*Sybil*, III, ix)

Gerard's response ('It is all very fine . . . and I dare say you are right, Stephen; but I like stretching my feet on my own hearth') is meant to set at nought all Morley's theories by a simple appeal to domestic comfort. In fact, Morley is generally portrayed by Disraeli with a certain amount of irony, if not sarcasm. We note that Harold, the Saxon bloodhound, does not like him, and when Mr Nixon the miner tells him 'you speak like a book', we are left in no doubt that Stephen Morley's dreams are considered by the author to be insubstantial. As the novel progresses, indeed, we become more and more irritated by Morley's outbursts. His exclamation to Sybil that 'We are all born for love . . . It is the principle of existence, and its only end', when he is trying to woo her, seems incongruous, for nowhere previously has he hinted that his ideas have anything to do with love. The fact that we have to make such a comment is itself indicative of Morley's 'character', for nothing in the novel suggests that he is a figure capable of feeling love for an *individual*. Thus it is that, in judging Morley, we are only really judging a collection of nineteenth-century 'communist' axioms – and in these, at least, Disraeli had no faith.

If the British political system is to be a redeeming feature in future society, Disraeli obviously intends that the House of Commons (and the House of Lords) should be stocked with such men as Charles Egremont. As a character Egremont has to undergo a process of learning that, however unconvincing at times, is not allowed to most of the other figures. This process begins in his travels abroad that we hear about. But, at the same time, he is presented as a man with a will independent enough to cause domestic and political comment, and as someone with an aim (we are never told *what* it is exactly) which, in its seeming reliance on existing class divisions, is seen to be not only legitimate but also practicable.

Even when we hear him betting on the Derby at the very beginning of the book, we hear that 'he would trust his star, he would not hedge' – a remark that is presumably meant to be prophetic. Of course, Egremont's resolutions and altruistic ambitions are helped in no small degree, it is implied, by his education at Eton and Christ Church, a background which has never been known to prejudice the Tory Party unfavourably against the individual concerned. When we hear he has a clever and influential mother as well, we begin to wonder whether young Mr Charles might not have 'got on' without any hint of interest or ability on his own part. Nevertheless, Egremont is supposed to be a potential messiah for the 'true' aristocracy, or at least representative of a messianic deliverance. As he says to Sybil,

> There is a dayspring in the history of this nation which those who are on the mountain tops can as yet perhaps only recognize. You deem you are in darkness, and I see a dawn. The new generation of the aristocracy of England are not tyrants, nor oppressors, Sybil, as you persist in believing. Their intelligence, better than that, their hearts are open to the responsibility of their position. But the work that is before them is no holiday-work. It is not the fever of superficial impulse that can remove the deep-fixed barriers of centuries of ignorance and crime. Enough that their sympathies are awakened; time and thought will bring the rest. They are the natural leaders of the People, Sybil; believe me they are the only ones. (*Sybil*, IV, xv)

Significantly it is Sybil that Disraeli and Egremont have to persuade – significantly if only because she is such an unworldly character that we find ourselves thinking that the knowledge she requires is considerably more than what is suggested; namely, that all will be all right when the poor, misled girl realises that there is not an unbridgeable gap between the aristocrats and the workers.

From the beginning her nature is rather inhuman, even spectral: 'Egremont might for a moment have been pardoned for believing her a seraph, that had lighted on this sphere, or the fair phantom of some saint haunting the sacred ruins of her desecrated fane.' Even Walter Gerard, her father, admits that 'Sybil knows nothing of the real world except its sufferings'. Throughout the novel we find this untouchable and untouched 'do-gooder' heroine drifting from one scene to the next, apparently unscathed, and it is perhaps to be expected that her whole aspect smacks of self-righteousness:

> The quick intelligence and the ardent imagination of Sybil had made her comprehend with fervour the two ideas that had been impressed on her young mind; the oppression of her church and the degradation

of her people. Educated in solitude and exchanging thoughts only with individuals of the same sympathies, these impressions had resolved themselves into one profound and gloomy conviction, that the world was divided only between the oppressors and the oppressed. With her, to be one of the people, was to be miserable and innocent; one of the privileged, a luxurious tyrant. In the cloister, in her garden, amid the scenes of suffering which she often visited and always solaced, she had raised up two phantoms which with her represented human nature. (*Sybil*, V, i)

This attitude finds frequent voice; for example, 'Oh, sir!...I am one of those who believe the gulf is impassable', and 'The dove and the eagle will not mate; the lion and the lamb will not lie down together; and the conquerors will never rescue the conquered'. The outbursts from such a faceless 'seraph' threaten to become irritating (especially when we find out that she is an aristocrat), and we condemn her apparent narrowness, as Disraeli wants us to, but without ever really bothering to take her prejudices seriously. If this is an example of characterisation giving way to some kind of thematic insistence, it is also an example of how thematic insistence becomes uninteresting in Disraeli when 'character', caricature, flamboyance and humour are absent.

Part of the reason, however, why such failings do not harm the book irreparably is that there is always a strong sense of fabular morality in Disraeli's presentation. For example, we have the Saxon qualities of Harold the bloodhound, the idyllic nature of Walter Gerard's garden, the parallel between Sybil and the young Queen Victoria, Egremont's assuming the name of 'Franklin', and Lord Valentine's suit of armour – a symbol of past greatness, present insularity and future fancy-dress balls. The fact that such symbolic moments do not become tiresome in themselves is due, to a large extent, to Disraeli's pervasive irony which can switch easily from a joking reference to a sour prophecy. In the light of this fabular quality we are entitled to ask what has been gained within the world of the novel. After all, the wheel seems to have come full circle – we have one Lord Marney at the beginning of the novel, and another one at the end. Does it really matter to society at large that the person underneath the title is different? Disraeli obviously believed it did; but it is a point made more pertinent by Chaffing Jack's philosophy that 'the name's everything', no matter what the commodity. Whether it be calling an American a 'colonel' to quieten him down in a bar, or whether it be Morley's title of 'The Secretary of the Mowbray Temperance and Teetotal', 'the name's everything'. In fact, the names and titles of people are considered so important by the society that Disraeli presents that they can justify the existence of a man like Baptist Hatton, and it is difficult to know just where the author's irony stops and where his true beliefs begin. Could it be that the question of the Two Nations, and its answer, are a mere points of rhetoric in terms of the world of the novel? Patrick Brantlinger has found the book wanting in this respect, 'for instead of containing a pattern of genuine paradoxes leading to Tory-radicalism as a climactic oxymoron, *Sybil* contains only a skein of contradictions, growing out of its conflicting plots of the educations of hero and heroine'.[11] This is a valid criticism of the novel as a thesis in isolation, but it does not fully take into account the place of *Sybil* in a tradition of works which all reflect the skein of contradictions in Disraeli's life. Disraeli's view of the human condition, even if it reflects mainly the author's own idiosyncrasies, is ultimately more significant for an assessment of the man as a novelist than is any attempt to construct a philosophical and political synthesis through fiction. Perhaps the most important oxymoron to be remembered is that of 'political novelist'.

Notes: Chapter 6

1   For Disraeli's treatment of rural problems see Martin Fido, 'The treatment of rural distress in Disraeli's *Sybil*', *Yearbook of English Studies*, vol. 5 (1975).

2   *Dombey and Son*, ch. 55.

3   *Autobiography* (1883), p. 163; *The Old Curiosity Shop* (1841), ch. 34; *Sybil*, III, i.

4   'Tommy' was the name given to goods and provisions supplied to workers under the 'truck' system. Instead of always receiving money for their wages, the workers were allowed a certain amount of credit at the 'tommy-shop'. This shop was often owned by a local employer who not only charged higher prices than the independent shops, but was also able, in practice, to force workers to accept, in lieu of wages, commodities they might not want.

5   Joseph E. Baker, *The Novel and the Oxford Movement* (Princeton, NJ: Princeton University Press, 1932), pp. 45–53.

6   Patrick Brantlinger, *The Spirit of Reform* (London: Harvard University Press, 1977), p. 102.

7   The demands of the Chartists: universal male suffrage, equal electoral districts, ballot voting, annually elected Parliaments, the payment of members of Parliament and the abolition of the property qualification for membership. Only five points were mentioned on the petition presented to Parliament by the Chartists; the demand for equal electoral districts was left out.

8   For a study of *Sybil* from the point of view of its Chartist content see Brantlinger.

9   Richard Monckton Milnes, as mentioned in the previous chapter, was generally sympathetic to Young England. He was the model for Mr Vavasour in *Tancred*.

10 Review of *Tancred* in the July number of the *Edinburgh Review* for 1847, quoted by Robert Blake, *Disraeli* (London: Eyre & Spottiswoode, 1966), pp. 206–7.

11 Brantlinger, p. 101.

7

Spells of Social Sorcery

On 27 November 1847 George Eliot wrote to Sara Sophia Hennell: 'I am provoked with you for being in the least pleased with Tancred, but if you have found out any lofty meaning in it or any true picturing of life, tell it me and I will recant.'[1] George Eliot did not recant, and it would hardly be an overstatement to say that most readers of the novel since it was published in March 1847 have found in it neither lofty meaning nor true picturing to any great extent. *Tancred, or, The New Crusade* was the final part of Disraeli's so-called Young England trilogy. It was also the least successful financially, and is, in almost every respect, a lesser book than either *Coningsby* or *Sybil*.

It has too often been assumed that Disraeli conceived of these three novels as forming a distinct trilogy, isolated within his *oeuvre* by a clear philosophy and shared aims. What is not often realised is that Disraeli first publicly presented his novels of the 1840s in this context only in 1849, in the preface to the fifth edition of *Coningsby*. The fact that he repeated this conceptual view of these works throughout the rest of his life (most notably in the general preface which introduced the collected edition of his novels published in 1870) has often led critics to take him at his word. However, it would seem clear that in his retrospective assessments of his literary works, Disraeli both desired, and was able, to organise and order those expressions which were governed as much by impulse and contemporary events as they were by any far-sighted plan. Even if we accept Disraeli's claim to have anticipated the end of *Tancred* when he was at his desk in 1844 writing *Coningsby*, it is still legitimate to question the *direction* which the trilogy took in relation to those three very hectic years of the author's life.

By 1849, when Disraeli was a front-bench politician aspiring to a front-bench political respectability, he was obviously interested in accentuating the political and topical contexts of novels which had been criticised for their affectations and romantic illusions as much as for their 'ideas'.

In the preface to the fifth edition of *Coningsby* he said:

> It was not originally the intention of the writer to adopt the form of
> fiction as the instrument to scatter his suggestions, but, after reflec-
> tion, he resolved to avail himself of a method which, in the temper of
> the times, offered the best chance of influencing opinion.

It is a view which seems at first genuine enough. After all, as we have
seen, Isaac D'Israeli had used the same argument in launching his
novel *Vaurien* in 1797, when he said in the preface that he had chosen
the *form* of a novel rather than the *matter*. But there is also a slight disingenuousness in Benjamin's words fifty-two years later. He had
already attempted to foist some of his unorthodox political views on
the world in 1835 when he published his *Vindication*. Whether or not
Disraeli's view of *Coningsby* and *Sybil* was shaped in any substantial
way by the public reception of the *Vindication* is something we can
only guess at. Certainly, the 1840s saw Disraeli expressing his views in
speeches as well as fiction, and there is no hint that he felt his own
rhetorical oratory to be anything less than penetrating and effective.
The 1840s were a time of 'propagandist' novels. Mrs Gaskell's *Mary
Barton* appeared in 1848 and Charles Kingsley's *Yeast* and *Alton
Locke* in 1848 and 1850 respectively. Probably more important, however, as an expression of the Victorian conscience, were the works of
Carlyle. *Chartism* was published in 1839 and *Past and Present* in 1843,
and both were relevant to the themes explored in Disraeli's Young
England novels. Disraeli may never have read Carlyle, but he certainly
could not have been anything other than very aware of the seer's
influence on mid-nineteenth-century opinion. Disraeli was not, after
all, appealing in his novels to that expanding middle-class which
adored Dickens. The 'opinion' which Disraeli was seeking to influence
might well have been *more* persuaded had the author's ideas not been
swathed in fictional garb. The fact is that Disraeli enjoyed writing
stories and creating worlds he could manipulate, as much as he enjoyed
persuading people of the verity of his views.

  'Enjoyment', however, was not always a comfortable companion of
Victorian *gravitas* or earnestness. The general preface of 1870,
although acknowledging the importance of imagination in political
matters, was at pains to stress the serious and well-ordered intention of
the trilogy. His aims, in retrospect, seem very symmetrical and
complementary:

> The derivation and character of political parties; the condition of the
> people which had been the consequence of them; the duties of the
> Church as a main remedial agency in our present state; were the
> principal topics which I intended to treat, but I found they were too
> vast for the space I had allotted to myself.

They were all launched in 'Coningsby' but the origin and condition of political parties, the first portion of the theme, was the only one completely handled in that work.

Next year (1845), in SYBIL, OR THE TWO NATIONS, I considered the condition of the people, and the whole work, generally speaking, was devoted to that portion of my scheme...

In recognizing the Church as a powerful agent in the previous development of England...it seemed to me that the time had arrived when it became my duty to...consider the position of the descendants of that race who had been the founders of Christianity. Familiar as we all are now with such themes, the House of Israel being now freed from the barbarism of medieval misconception, and judged like other races by their contributions to the existing sum of human welfare, and the general influence of race on human action being universally recognized as the key of history, the difficulty and hazard of touching for the first time on such topics cannot now be easily appreciated. But public opinion recognized both the truth and sincerity of these views, and with its sanction, in TANCRED OR THE NEW CRUSADE, the third portion of the Trilogy, I completed their development.

For several reasons, *Tancred* looks uncomfortable alongside *Coningsby* and *Sybil*; it was, indeed, both more and less than a natural progression from the other two novels. If Disraeli did recognise in *Coningsby* and *Sybil* the church as 'a powerful agent' in the development of England, then in *Tancred* he attempted to theorise and expand on its remedial possibilities. However, much of the novel is set in a geographically abstracted environment (the Near East) and it is difficult not to feel that the original dilemma also becomes abstracted and dislocated. For all the hero's apparent adventures, the novel does not suggest that the experience gained from them will easily transfer into the English social system with any beneficial effect.

Part of the reason for the isolated nature of *Tancred* was Disraeli's own political position. *Coningsby* and *Sybil* were, if not entirely motivated by Young England sympathies, at least excusable as expressions of a back-bench politician. In their dealings with parliamentary matters and the 'condition of England' question, they were viewed as legitimate, albeit unusual, extensions of the novelist's canon. After 1846 and the fall from office of Peel, in which of course the novelist had been prominent, Disraeli was in a completely new position. Not only was Young England dead, but, more important, Disraeli had no further desire to flaunt his unconventionality. As we shall see, on the matter of religion he was still determined to make a principled stand, even if his political position were to be somewhat jeopardised as a result of it. There is no sense, then, in regarding *Tancred* as insincere. What seems far more likely is that in this novel Disraeli was expressing something which was instinctively and intellectually nearer to his heart than either the relationship of class and party allegiances in *Coningsby* or the industrial malpractices of *Sybil*. Nevertheless, the fact that much of the novel is set in a distant geographical locality meant that it was to a certain extent distanced from Disraeli's political career. The Disraeli of 1847 was, both by necessity and by shrewd calculation, more 'respectable' than the Disraeli of one or two years earlier. When Parliament reassembled on 19 January 1847 he sat for the first time on the front bench, albeit of the opposition, in the House of Commons. He no longer wore his usual bright colours and gold chains, and his flamboyant manner had largely disappeared. Instead he sat in a very composed way, dressed in a sober black suit. When he stood up to speak, his tone was as deliberate as ever, but he avoided the high-flown and impassioned phrases which had marked his earlier speeches, especially those of 1846 when he was concentrating all his invective against Peel. Although it was not perhaps obvious at the time, Disraeli the novelist was entering a period of hibernation; it was to be twenty-three years before another novel was published under his name.

In retrospect, then, *Tancred* completed an era, although, as we shall see, when Disraeli was writing *Lothair* the lengthy gap between the novels was not always apparent. Mainly for the reasons already outlined, *Tancred* was not as successful as *Coningsby* and *Sybil* (nor has it been ever since). It sold 2,500 copies and Disraeli earned from it about £750. However, the reader of either *Coningsby* or *Sybil*, on coming fresh to *Tancred*, is usually delighted by its opening. The first pages of the novel are among the best Disraeli wrote, and they are full of colour, wit and movement. Geographically Disraeli is 'at home' here, in an aristocratic quarter of London. The phraseology is familiar: Prevost says to Mr Leander 'Gaillard and Abreu will not serve under you, eh? And if they would, they could not be trusted. They would betray you at the tenth hour.' It is the phraseology of the politician, except here it is applied to the hierarchy of cooking and the catering arrangements that Mr Leander has been commissioned to make. Once again Disraeli appears to be 'at home' with food, and we see the artist creating his world with unmistakable relish.

From this beginning the novel fans out to cover much of the metropolitan parliamentary and social scene, and as the many personages are paraded before us as if at a cocktail party, we are aware of Disraeli's efforts to impose on the work a superficial link with *Coningsby* and *Sybil* which the rest of *Tancred* only thinly supports. This is achieved mainly through the use of characters from the earlier books. Sidonia reappears and has some genuine impact on the plans of the young Tancred. But the presence of Coningsby and Egremont (now, of course, Lord Marney), and several other names from the earlier novels, does little to impress us with any feeling of continuity. Abstracted from their own philosophical dilemmas which motivated their respective fictional vehicles, the revived Coningsby and Egremont are faint copies of the faint originals. Coningsby, we remember, had sacrificed money for principles only to end up with both. The older Coningsby is obviously more calculating now that he has his fortune: he 'looked to a great fortune as one of the means, rightly employed, of obtaining great power'. In the interests of Young England it is no great surprise to find that 'Political sympathy had created a close intimacy between Lord Marney and Coningsby', but it is interesting to see what has happened to the aspirations of the group. *Tancred* is the only one of the three novels to mention Young England overtly – a fact made easier because by 1847 it was all history. It had served its purpose by providing an idealised colouring to the opposition which had been mounting against Peel in the early 1840s. The energy of Lord Henry Sidney, for example, was now channelled into every possible legitimate source of political activity:

> The debate, the committee, the article in the Journal or the Review, the public meeting, the private research – these were all means to advance that which he had proposed as the object of his public life, namely, to elevate the condition of the people. (*Tancred*, II, xiii)

No doubt Disraeli the politician would have heartily approved of this selfless application; but there is a hint that Disraeli the novelist regrets the loss of that different kind of energy which marked out Lord Henry and Coningsby at Eton and Cambridge.

It was suggested in Chapter 5 that, for all his emphasis on individual character, Disraeli realised that this could only be successful as a salvationary factor in society if it were itself a reflection of what was loosely termed the 'national character'. In *Tancred* this idea is again central, and it provides the one sustaining link with *Coningsby*. This is partly because most of the apposite expressions ('What is individual character but the personification of race . . . its perfection and choice exemplar?') come from the lips of Sidonia. His very un-Englishness, which served to widen and universalise the young Coningsby's ideals, serves, in *Tancred*, as a kind of symbol of the adventure and knowledge which awaits Tancred in the East. The fact that Sidonia is also at the heart of Western capitalism proves no difficulty for Disraeli: it is another one of his idiosyncrasies. (Sometimes the word 'paradox' is too flattering; the word 'inconsistency' too demeaning.) His amazing wealth allows Disraeli the continued pleasure of describing those details which were for him an integral part of the social scene:

> At present the dinner was served on Sevres porcelain of Rose de Berri, raised on airy golden stands of arabesque workmanship; a mule bore your panniers of salt, or a sea-nymph proffered it you on a shell just fresh from the ocean, or you found it in a bird's nest; by every guest a

different pattern. In the centre of the table, mounted on a pedestal, was a group of pages in Dresden china. Nothing could be more gay than their bright cloaks and flowing plumes, more elaborately exquisite than their laced shirts and rosettes, or more fantastically saucy than their pretty affected faces, as each, with extended arm, held a light to a guest. (*Tancred*, II, xiv)

There is no heavy irony here (as there is, for example, in Dickens's presentation of the Veneerings' table decoration in *Our Mutual Friend*, I, ii); Disraeli is too obviously enjoying the trappings of a Rothschildish world which can best be glimpsed today through the interiors of Waddesdon Manor. But Sidonia is not only viewed through the effects of fashionable European society. He is also given in *Tancred*, through stories related about him, another dimension which goes back to his experiences in the East. It is one aspect of his past which sounds highly improbable. Baroni's proverbial morality in the novel is based to a great extent on his past adventures with Sidonia: 'he who gains time gains everything, as M. de Sidonia said to me when the savages were going to burn us alive, and there came on a thunderstorm which extinguished their fagots'. The thought of Sidonia ever being in a situation where he might be burned alive seems somewhat less than credible, but the interpolation of such stories does at least mean that he is a tangible link between the East and the West which Tancred can always keep in mind.

Tancred's own movement is one from West End saloons to adventures in the desert, and in the context of Disraeli's earlier novels it is not unusual to see the hero shunning convention for an exploration which is not only geographical, but also spiritual and psychological. (The link with *Contarini Fleming* is made explicit through the character of Besso, who appears in both novels.) Tancred's arguments are individual in that they are against having faith in Parliament: 'Parliament seems to me', he tells Lord Henry Sidney, 'to be the very place which a man of action should avoid.' Tancred fulfils the dream of being a man of action when he becomes a military leader later in the book. His action reflects a freedom of expression and a selfless commitment to principles which, despite their romanticised nature, represent for Disraeli much of the Eastern way of life. For the modern reader, however, Disraeli's Eastern picture is most easily remembered by the idioms which characterise the speech of the Arabs, as in 'May your mother eat the hump of a young camel!' or 'One grape will not make a bunch, even though it be a great one'. In the midst of such an Eastern scene, Tancred's position seems slightly absurd:

In this strange and splendid scene, Tancred, dressed in a velvet shooting-jacket built in St. James's-street and a wide-awake which had been purchased at Bellamont market, and leaning on a rifle which was the masterpiece of Purday, was not perhaps the least interesting personage. (*Tancred*, V ii)

While Tancred represents a principled and idealised youthful England in search of Eastern mysteries, the Arab world's most 'energetic' ambassador in the novel is Fakredeen, another young man:

> Fakredeen possessed all the qualities of the genuine Syrian character in excess; vain, susceptible, endowed with a brilliant though frothy imagination, and a love of action so unrestrained that restlessness deprived it of energy, with so fine a taste that he was always capricious, and so ingenious that he seemed ever inconsistent.

On one level Fakredeen is presented as being the opposite of the admirable Tancred, with whom the reader might have been expected to identify. In this respect Fakredeen is a character of many limitations. But as the description just quoted suggests, there is also much of him which reflects the 'frothy' side of Disraeli. Disraeli is therefore not without some admiration for Fakredeen, although it is an admiration for qualities which the author would not readily have admitted:

> he lived in the centre in intrigues which were to shake thrones, and perhaps to form them. He became habituated to the idea that everything could be achieved by dexterity, and that there was no test of conduct except success. To dissemble and to simulate; to conduct confidential negotiations with contending powers and parties at the same time; to be ready to adopt any opinion and to possess none; to fall into the public humour of the moment and to evade the impending catastrophe; to look upon every man as a tool, and never to do anything which had not a definite though circuitous purpose – these were his political accomplishments; and, while he recognized them as the best means of success, he found in their exercise excitement and delight. To be the centre of a maze of manoeuvres was his empyrean. He was never without a resource. (*Tancred*, III, vi)

Disraeli, however, even if he could appreciate tactical advantages in such a political creed, was not so naive or unprincipled as not to acknowledge its failings, and Fakredeen is progressively shown as shallow and wrong-headed. Despite the explicit evocation of 'Young Syria' to mirror Young England, and despite the insistence on the 'two nations' of the Druses and Maronites, the parallels between Fakredeen's situation and any English problem is artistic rather than real. Tancred himself tries to disabuse Fakredeen of his ideas, stressing the limitations and unprincipled nature of the latter's 'intrigue'. It is a view Tancred feels confident of propounding on the basis of his status as a European new to the Arab world. But it is not, of course, as a soldier or a saviour that Tancred comes to the East. His main quest is for spiritual insight – the knowledge which he believes God has not spoken to a European. As he says,

> In England, when I prayed in vain for enlightenment, I at last induced myself to believe that the Supreme Being would not deign to reveal his will unless in the land which his presence had rendered holy; but since I have been a dweller within its borders, and poured forth my passionate prayers at all its holy places, and received no sign, the desolating thought has sometimes come over my spirit, that there is a qualification of blood as well as of locality necessary for this communion, and that the favoured votary must not only kneel in the Holy Land but be of the holy race. (*Tancred*, IV, iii)

Disraeli's idiosyncratic ideas on Christianity and Judaism form a subject in its own right, and there is not space here to attempt a full exploration of the way those ideas manifested themselves in both his fiction and his life. The crux of those beliefs was that Christianity was a completed form of Judaism. Tancred says:

> Through Jesus, God spoke to the Gentiles, and not to the tribes of Israel only. That is the great worldly difference between Jesus and his inspired precedessors. Christianity is Judaism for the multitude, but still it is Judaism . . . (*Tancred*, VI, iv)

As with Sidonia's speeches on race in *Coningsby*, it is another attempt by Disraeli to vindicate and rationalise his own Jewish descent and his adopted creed. It is another case of the paradox straining under the weight of its own inconsistencies, and it is a theme which can only really be expressed through the novelist's use of a somewhat superficial cleverness: 'Pray are you of those Franks who worship a Jewess; or of those others who revile her, break her images, and blaspheme her pictures?' The Jews are applauded for crucifying Christ in that by so doing they helped to instigate the Atonement, and the overall message of *Tancred* is that the Jews, who had suffered so much persecution, are the real saviours of the human race.

As suggested, Disraeli's ideas on Christianity and Judaism were mainly the result of his own ambivalent position and heritage. It is certainly not the only example of Disraeli constructing a philosophical and historical framework so as to be able to assimilate his own position. However, odd as they may be, Disraeli seems to have regarded his religious ideas with a conviction which is often absent from other aspects of his world picture. Four years after *Tancred* was published, in *Lord George Bentinck* in 1851, he again expressed the view that the Jews were the holy race who, through the crucifixion of one of their own kind, had saved the world.

Within the same year which saw the publication of *Tancred*,

Disraeli's religious principles were to be seen in a practical and political light. The general election of June 1847, three months after the appearance of *Tancred*, gave rise to a situation which was embarrassing for the new front-bench Disraeli. One of the newly elected Liberal members for the City of London was Baron Lionel de Rothschild who was, of course, a Jew. At that time the parliamentary oath had to be taken 'on the true faith of a Christian', which naturally excluded all Jews from taking their seats. While the Prime Minister, Lord John Russell, and the Liberals were keen to remove this bar, the majority of the Tory members felt it their duty to conserve the Christian character of a legislative body which was ultimately responsible for the doctrine and conduct of the Church of England. When, on 16 December, Russell moved that the House consider the removal of the Jewish civil disabilities, Disraeli chose to follow his conscience rather than the general feeling of his own party.

If his support for Russell had been in the name of religious toleration, the matter might not have seemed so extraordinary, even though *Tancred* had forewarned the public of Disraeli's unusual beliefs. As it was, Disraeli chose to speak out for the Jews on the same grounds of faith which governed his novel. His speech on the subject was an elucidation of belief; it did not seek to be either theologically liberal or politically non-committal: 'Yes it is as a Christian that I will not take upon me the awful responsibility of excluding from the Legislature those who are of the religion in the bosom of which my Lord and Saviour was born.'[2] There is no doubt, though, that despite Disraeli's avowal of his own faith, many of the Tory MPs who sat behind him were alarmed by his, perhaps unconscious, references to '*your* Christianity'. Most of them voted against Russell's motion, although their opposition could not prevent its being carried by a large majority. That did not, of course, mean that Baron Lionel could take his seat; the problem was to occupy Parliament intermittently for ten years, as various Jewish Emancipation Bills were carried in the House of Commons but rejected in the House of Lords. Whatever one's opinion of Disraeli's religious views as they affect his fiction, one cannot but applaud his defence of such views at the centre of public debate at a time when his political position was far from established. Any admiration, however, must stem from a respect for his outspokenness, rather than for his religious principles, which, though superficially ordered and presentable in a fictitious context, were at least hazy, and more usually incoherent. In one of his less serious moments, he is reported to have claimed that 'I am the blank page between the Old and the New Testament'. Such idiosyncratic wit is perhaps as relevant to an understanding of *Tancred* as is any study of Disraeli's religious heritage.

Once Disraeli was on the front bench of the House of Commons, his career as a novelist, through the pressure of circumstance and through intention, took a secondary place in his life. The transition to the front bench which was marked by a change in clothing and speech, was also set in high relief by the advent of several other incidents. During the winter of 1848 Disraeli and Mary Anne moved into Hughenden Manor, their newly acquired country residence just outside High Wycombe, which was to be his home for the rest of his life. He was now very much a man of affairs, a county member of Parliament and a country squire. Links with the past were fast falling away. On 21 April 1847 his mother had died at the age of 71. On 19 January of the following year Isaac followed her. Disraeli had always been very fond of his father, and was a great admirer of his literary talent. Bradenham, however, had not been owned by the D'Israelis. With Isaac's death ended Benjamin's attachment to that house which had seen and nurtured many of his own literary endeavours. The large library of 25,000 books, which had been the frequent resort of the emerging novelist, was sold at Sotheby's. So much of what represented Disraeli's youth seemed now broken up, but his father was never forgotten; in 1866 when Disraeli was dining with Lord Stanley at Bellamy's the two of them drank a bottle of champagne in celebration of Isaac's birth one hundred years before.

If much of the past was still a charming remembrance for Disraeli, there were also incidents in his history which he would now have to try hard to live down. One of the Tory whips, Charles Newdegate, was still able to say of his colleague,

> I have been warned repeatedly not to trust Disraeli, while I see nothing in his public conduct to justify the want of confidence so many seem to feel. This I conclude is attributable to some circumstances of his earlier life with which I am not familiar . . . I can scarcely help believing there must be some foundation for so general an opinion as I have alluded to, and it makes me very uneasy.[3]

Those 'some circumstances' included every public extravagance in Disraeli's life from *Vivian Grey* to his opinions on the Jewish question. Disraeli managed to overcome prejudice by sheer application and hard work, although he was never to escape fully the reputation of his youthful activities. Another Tory whip, William Beresford, wrote of Disraeli in September 1849: 'He is living very quietly and working very hard. He is reading up all the Blue Books of the past session . . . He attributes Peel's great power and effect in the House to having always had Blue Books by heart, and having thereby the appearance of a fund of greater knowledge than he really possessed.'[4] It is interesting that Disraeli, only three years after he had been instrumental in the fall of Peel, should be keen to emulate some of the qualities of his former adversary. Such an attitude was in accordance with the move from back-bench flamboyance to front-bench responsibility.

The only obvious ties between such sedulous research and the life of the novelist seems to be in the Blue Books themselves, which, as noted, formed a major influence in the composition of *Sybil*. But perhaps such an observation calls for a comparison of Disraeli's views of matters which featured in both his fictional and political worlds. Lord Ashley's Ten Hours Act of 1847 had had several loopholes which meant that employers had been able to exploit factory workers beyond the ten hours a day originally envisaged by the supporters of the measure. In 1850 Ashley introduced a new Factories Bill which was intended to tighten up the former legislation, and the author of *Sybil* lent his support in a gesture which, if not strictly parallel with that concerning the Jewish question, did at least seem to be an instance of Disraeli applying his fictional precepts to political fact. However, on the question of coal mines, Disraeli the novelist's philosophical radicalism was to give way to political expediency, and when a Bill was proposed advocating the inspection of mines, he voted against it in the House of Commons. There is no point in making excuses for Disraeli by avoiding the simple truth that factory owners tended to be Liberals and coal owners tended to be Tories.

His only major literary work between the publication of *Tancred* and the writing of *Lothair* was *Lord George Bentinck: A Political Biography*, which, although bearing the date 1852, appeared in December 1851. Unlike most of Disraeli's novels, *Lord George Bentinck* cannot be understood and appreciated without a knowledge both of the book's subject and of its political background. There are many passages in the biography, both on and off the subject of Bentinck himself, which have always been found by critics to be very quotable, and they contribute very much to our overall picture of Disraeli. A major example is the long discursion on the Jewish race, which has already been mentioned. But from the point of view of examining Disraeli the novelist, *Lord George Bentinck* is mainly interesting as an example of the author's willingness to tackle most forms of literary and political expression, and is a tribute to the great affection and respect he had for Bentinck.

Disraeli only got to know Bentinck in those months which led up to the final onslaught on Peel's administration over the Corn Laws. The two men could have hardly been more different; yet together they proved to be too much for Peel and his followers. Despite his obvious lack of parliamentary genius, Bentinck had seemed destined to play an important part in the realignment of political sympathies after 1846, but on 21 September 1848 he died suddenly of a heart attack whilst out walking alone. Disraeli's efforts to commemorate his colleague with a biography were immediate and were spurred on by a genuine sense of loss and a feeling of respect, rather than by any literary or political opportunism. However, as with much of Disraeli's output, the biography is marked by excess, and while that is sometimes a great enhancing feature, it is also a limitation of the work as a serious contribution to history. Ultimately, the book tells us more about Disraeli than it does about Bentinck. The relation of the Corn Law debates, for example, is brought to vivid life by Disraeli's extravagant style, and in this respect the work is still very much a necessity for any student of this period of history. But the eulogy of Bentinck itself is too unrestrained; while below the superficial wording of the praise, the study's ostensible subject remains sketchy, we are reminded rather of the author's perpetual flamboyance. Disraeli underplays considerably his own role in the fall of Peel, but it is *his* energy which stares from every page.

The book was widely praised on its publication, except by those Tories who noticed that it hardly mentioned Derby at all. Despite Bentinck's temporary prominence in the House of Commons, Lord Derby had been the acknowledged leader of the protectionist Tories as early as March 1846. Of course, with protection being such a touchy subject in 1852, Disraeli may have, consciously rather than unconsciously, been doing his leader a favour by underplaying his role as an antagonist of free trade. It would be difficult to think that Disraeli would have omitted to mention Derby's role in the fall of Peel for any other reason; as Robert Blake has aptly put it: 'With Disraeli history was not only past politics but present politics, too.'[5] As has already been seen, Disraeli was never one to deny himself the opportunity of reordering the past so as to make it fit more comfortably with the present.

During the early 1850s Disraeli was to have the chance to see his fiction in such an ordered way. In 1853, when Disraeli's name was at last well known throughout the country, David Bryce published a uniform edition of the novels. Disraeli must have looked forward to the prospect of an eager public buying his varied artistic achievements (each one of which was now produced in one volume), and indeed, apart from the much-appreciated money which the edition would secure, such a bulk publication would itself have been a sign of his new status. But on the other hand Disraeli had no desire to have his early indiscretions widely publicised at a time when he was a respected parliamentarian and a Cabinet minister. The edition was therefore to be a 'revised' one, and the revised texts were to form the basis of the 1870 collected edition issued by Longmans, which in turn provided the texts used by most subsequent editions.

As might have been expected, the most heavily revised texts were those of his early works, especially *Vivian Grey*. Revision of some kind or another had been going on ever since the novels were first published. For example, *Contarini Fleming*, which had appeared also with the heading 'A Psychological Auto-Biography', had had its subtitle changed soon after the publication of the first edition, to 'A Psychological Romance', in a revision which was obviously intended to make the novel appear rather more impersonal. The year of its publication, 1832, was, after all, the year in which Disraeli began his series of attempts to be elected to Parliament. So too with *Vivian Grey*, the revising had begun almost as soon as the novel's first edition appeared, and some of the changes were made for the second edition of 1826. More of the pruning, however, was done for the David Bryce version, and it is perhaps worth noting here the sort of passages which readers coming fresh to the famous Disraeli in 1853 would not have read. Most of the differences concerned social solecisms, for we must remember that when Disraeli wrote *Vivian Grey* he really knew nothing of high society or the conduct of dukes and marquises. But there were also changes which related directly to those aspects of his work which have been of particular interest to this study.

His attitude to his father, for example, which seems to have been ambivalent in his youth, had probably been reflected in this comment on Vivian Grey's father: 'a father is, perhaps, the worst judge of his son's capacity. He knows too much – and too little.' It certainly seems true that Isaac D'Israeli did not fully appreciate the talents of his most gifted son, and Benjamin Disraeli's original draft reflects his awareness of this. One can only assume that, having become a national figure after his father's death, Disraeli felt himself prompted to omit some of these slighting domestic references. It must also be said that such changes also contributed to Disraeli's restyling of his past which, as we have seen already, is nowhere more clear than in his censoring of certain passages which reflect on his schooldays.

Apart from the portrayal of the domestic situations which have interested modern biographers, *Vivian Grey* had in its time been most vilified for its presentation of well-known personages under thinly disguised caricatures. There had been slighting references to people like John Wilson Croker, and most of these did not appear in the version of 1853. But the main scandal had, of course, surrounded the similarity which readers had chosen to see between the Marquess of Carabas and John Murray, the publisher. Whether or not Disraeli was genuinely sorry for an indiscretion, or whether he was just being politic, all the references to the Marquess's tipsiness were omitted from the revised edition of the novel.

The overall intention of much of this censorship was to distance the author from his hero. It was an impossible task, for Disraeli had always been, and would always be, associated with Vivian Grey. But at least the leading politician was able to exorcise some of his narrator's more embarrassing frankness:

I am loath to speak even one moment of the author, instead of the hero; but with respect to those who have with such singular industry associated the character of the author of Vivian Grey with that of his hero; I must observe, that as this is an inconvenience which I share in company with more celebrated writers, so also is it one which will never prevent me from describing any character which my mind may conceive . . .

Of the personal, and political matter contained in the former books of this work, I can declare, that though written in a hasty, it was not written in a reckless spirit; and that there is nothing contained in those volumes of which I am morally ashamed (*Vivian Grey*, V, i)

This passage never appeared after 1853, except in purposeful reprints of the first edition, which were few. Another victim of the reviser's censorship was Disraeli's excessive delight in culinary matters which we have already noted throughout his early work. The original *Vivian Grey* had printed the following:

All kinds of cold meats, and all kinds of pasties, venison, pheasants, plovers, rabbits, pickled fish, prawns, and craw fish, greeted the ravished eyes of the wearied band of foresters. July is not a month for eating; but, nevertheless, in Germany we are somewhat consoled for the want of the curious varieties of cookery, by the exhilarating presence of white young partridges, delicious ducklings, and most tender leverets. Then there were all sorts of forced meats, and stuffed birds. You commenced with a pompous display of unnecessary science, to extract for a famished fair one the wing and merry-thought of a fairer chicken – when lo, and behold! the facile knife sunk without an effort into the plump breast, and the unresisting bird discharged a cargo of rich stuffed balls, of the most fascinating flavour.

However, most readers of the novel have missed such sensuous description. The Bryce edition, and nearly all subsequent editions, produced instead a description of a table which

glowed with materials, and with colours to which Veronese alone could have done justice; pasties and birds, and venison, and groups of fish, glowing with prismatic lines.

It was the excesses and the solecisms which were cut from *The Young Duke* rather than anything topical or political. It was an attempt to prune away some of the flippancies which Bulwer had warned about more than twenty years earlier; although those references which contributed to Disraeli's cogent progression on the subject of jewellery were left untouched. With these early novels the 1853 changes bear the stamp of Disraeli's hand, but it must be remembered that the period leading up to the publication of the Bryce edition was one of unsurpassed political activity for Disraeli, as he gained office for the first time, as Chancellor of the Exchequer, and planned, presented and defended his first budget. It is not surprising then that much of the revision seems not to have been done by him personally. The Young England trilogy had been written and widely read while Disraeli was an MP and, six years after the publication of *Tancred*, there was little in it that Disraeli wished to suppress. Apart from anything else, his views on the Young England ideals and his own idiosyncratic ideas on race were already widely known. A comparison, therefore, between the first edition of *Sybil* and the revised edition shows a surprisingly small number of changes, other than those affecting punctuation and formal presentation. The urge to restyle his past effusions was still there, but it was now balanced by an appreciation of the realistic amount of attention that a hectic life in politics demanded. The next fifteen years were to be marked by insecure governments in Parliament, and it was a trying time for Disraeli as he sought to defend and consolidate his position as the leading Conservative in the House of Commons. Paradoxically, it was the great triumph of Gladstone in 1868 which indirectly accounted for Disraeli's re-emergence as a novelist.

Disraeli first held office, as Chancellor of the Exchequer, in 1851. His first budget came at an unlucky time, and proved to be the thing which ensured that the Liberals returned to power. For a man, then, whose entire life, literature and career had been characterised by the ambition of a leader, it must have been a severe disappointment to find himself so quickly returned to the opposition benches. Yet that year of influence was the basis on which his later rise to the premiership was founded. The Prime Minister in that short interlude had been Lord Derby, who led the country from the upper chamber. Disraeli had not only been Chancellor of the Exchequer, but also the Leader of the House of Commons. His status in the Commons was therefore considerable, and his prominent, albeit short, position in the government of the country meant that his name was now known throughout the land, rather than just in political and literary circles. The *Edinburgh Review*, in its first number for 1853, devoted a forty-page character sketch to the new national figure. As the writer of the sketch asked, 'What individual from February 1852 to January 1853 has most occupied the pens, tongues and ears of Englishmen?'[6] The answer was, of course, Disraeli, of whom the journal went on to say:

> His portrait was painted by one fashionable artist; his bust was taken in marble, *aere perennius*, by another; what were called likenesses of him appeared in illustrated newspapers by the dozen; and, above all, he was placed in Madame Tussaud's repository – that British Valhalla in which it is difficult for a civilian to gain a niche without being hanged.

Within the next three years two lives of Disraeli were to be published. G. M. Francis's *Critical Biography* could see nothing bad in its subject, and T. Macknight's *Literary and Political Biography* could see nothing good. Robert Blake's judgement that 'Both works are equally valueless to the historian, save as evidence of the vigour and diversity of the sentiments that Disraeli could inspire' is surely the correct one.

When Disraeli's pen was active after *Lord George Bentinck*, it was mainly engaged on contributions to journals. In this area he was spurred on not merely by opportunism and the remembrance of his youthful journalistic sallies, but rather by a political need. The Conservative Party of the 1850s could by no means count on anything like the press support which the Liberals had. It was a deficiency which had occupied the minds of Disraeli and Lord Stanley for a few years, and it led to the founding of the *Press* which first appeared on 7 May 1853. The *Press* was a weekly publication, and, far from being a strictly Conservative Party organ, was rather, to use Disraeli's words, 'of a very progressive and enlightened design'.[7] The contributors included Disraeli's old friends George Smythe and Bulwer Lytton, and Disraeli himself wrote many of the first leading articles, although he was at pains to continue his writing role in secret. His own last piece appeared in the *Press* in 1856, and two years later, when he found himself back in office, he sold the paper. While Disraeli's involvement with the publication was undoubtedly more successful than his endeavours to get the *Representative* off the ground thirty years earlier, it is interesting to note how, while holding a position of great responsibility in the House of Commons, he still managed to indulge his perennial taste for the unorthodox.

But if Disraeli's life continued to show signs of the secretive conniving which marked his early career and fictions, there were also signs that he was becoming an acceptable and respected figure in those circles which had not previously played an active role in his life. During 1853, for example, Oxford University, the place he had notably failed to attend as a youth, conferred on him an honorary DCL. The honour was due largely to Lord Derby who, while Prime Minister, had been elected chancellor of the university; but it was certainly an award which had a great deal of support among the undergraduates. They gave him a warm reception at both the Sheldonian Theatre and Christ Church, after the traditional gaudy, and there is no reason to think that Disraeli was anything other than sincerely grateful for this final recognition by the institution which had nurtured so many budding prime ministers within its walls.'

These years between 1853 and 1870 were obviously marked more by Disraeli's political achievements than by any literary predispositions; yet it is an intriguing comment on the link between the two areas of activity, that the Cabinet of 1858 contained two romantic novelists. It is perhaps not surprising that such a phenomenon had never occurred before and has never occurred since. On this occasion Disraeli was again Chancellor of the Exchequer, and his long-standing friend and colleague, now Bulwer Lytton, had control of the Colonial Office. The author of *Pelham* was by now deaf and therefore somewhat less than effective in parliamentary debates, but he was still a celebrity, and the presence of him and Disraeli in the administration helped to give Lord Derby's government some character.

But if Bulwer Lytton's place in the upper echelons of government was questionable, Disraeli's was certainly not, and in those years when he was not writing novels he displayed a great grasp of political realities. What is more, in a time of unsure parliamentary allegiances, he 'survived' – a not inconsiderable achievement. His most famous political enterprise at this time was, of course, the Reform Bill of 1867. It is not the intention of this study to devote time to the political career of Disraeli, which has obviously been covered more than adequately by his many biographers. But it is of some interest to the student of Disraeli the man and Disraeli the novelist to note once again the way in which, in life as in fiction, he blatantly restyled the past as it affected his own thesis, position and reputation. As is now accepted by historians, Disraeli can hardly be considered the architect of what finally emerged as the Reform Bill. He was, rather, responsible for the manoeuvring which had allowed the Bill to be shaped by several interests, and his claim later that he had been engaged in a planned act of 'educating' his party about reform has little basis in fact. It was also quite untrue that the Cabinet had been in favour of household suffrage since 1859, which he also claimed after the event. As Robert Blake has remarked: 'Disraeli contrived to put up, as most politicians do, a facade of consistency, but, in fact, he lived from crisis to crisis, improvising, guessing, responding to the mood of the moment.'[8] It is true that most politicians do this, but the reputation Disraeli acquired for being unscrupulous was, to a great extent, due to his application of that principle to literature and life in general. Through his novels, his revisions, his political satires and his overall interpretation of life, Disraeli had attempted to contribute in a very public way to 'a facade of consistency'.

Whatever the merits of such an attitude, Disraeli finally achieved what he had been striving after for so long. On 26 February 1868 Queen Victoria wrote to her daughter, the Crown Princess of Prussia:

> Mr. Disraeli is Prime Minister! A proud thing for a Man 'risen from the people' to have obtained! And I must say – really most loyally; it is his real talent, his good temper and the way in wh. he managed the Reform Bill last year – wh. have brought this about.[9]

The Disraelis celebrated at the end of March by giving a great reception at the Foreign Office, as Mary Anne considered Downing Street 'so dingy and decaying'. It was a very cold day, marked with sleet and snow, but even this could not prevent the novelist-cum-Prime Minister assembling in his honour a glittering party of notables worthy of one of the *levées* from the grandest of his fiction. The Prince and Princess of Wales were the main figures in a guest list which included dukes, bishops and ambassadors. Among the politicians present were leading lights of both sides of the House, including Gladstone and his wife. It was a moment to be seen as not only the culmination of many years of hard political work, but also as the fulfilment of an adventure which had been reflected in most of what Disraeli had written in his novels. As he had said in *Tancred* twenty years before,

> How full of adventure is life! It is monotonous only to the monotonous. There may be no longer fiery dragons, magic rings, or fairy wands, to interfere in its course and to influence our career; but the relations of men are far more complicated and numerous than of yore; and in the play of the passions, and in the devices of creative spirits, that have thus a proportionately greater sphere for their action, there are spells of social sorcery more potent than all the necromancy of Merlin or Friar Bacon. (*Tancred*, VI, viii)

The special brand of social sorcery had got Disraeli to the top of the greasy pole, but there were still more surprises in store. By the end of 1868 he was once more back on the opposition front bench. Politically 1869 was a quiet year for him. And then, on 2 May 1870, *Lothair* was published. To quote again the writer in the *Saturday Review*: 'Mr. Disraeli has provided a new sensation for a jaded public. The English mind was startled when a retired novelist became Prime Minister. It has been not less surprised at the announcement that a retired Prime Minister is about again to become a novelist.'

Notes: Chapter 7

1   Gordon S. Haight (ed.), *The George Eliot Letters* (London: Oxford University Press; New Haven, Conn.: Yale University Press, 1954), Vol. I, p. 241.
2   Quoted by Robert Blake, *Disraeli* (London: Eyre & Spottiswoode, 1966), p. 259.
3   Quoted in ibid., p. 265.
4   Quoted in ibid., p. 295.
5   ibid., p. 309.
6   Quoted in ibid., p. 349.
7   Quoted in ibid., p. 353.
8   ibid., p. 464.
9   Quoted in ibid., p. 487.

8

The Frame of Age

Two years before her letter to Sara Sophia Hennell on the subject of *Tancred*, George Eliot had written to Mrs Charles Bray on 25 May 1845: 'Tell Mr. Bray I received Sybil yesterday quite safely. I am not utterly disgusted with D'Israeli. The man hath good veins, as Bacon would say, but there is not enough blood in them.'[1] To a large extent, indeed, Disraeli's literary veins ran dry in the years before 1870 when *Lothair* was published. It could hardly be said that his talents as a novelist had been missed in those years while he was concentrating his energy into his political career. The period between the publication of *Sybil* and the appearance of *Lothair* was in many ways the most important one in the nineteenth century as far as English fiction was concerned. Mrs Gaskell's *Mary Barton* appeared in 1848, to be followed, among others, by *North and South* and *Wives and Daughters*. Charlotte Bronte's *Jane Eyre* and Emily's *Wuthering Heights* appeared in 1847. After the great success of *Vanity Fair* in 1847–8, Thackeray published *Pendennis, The History of Henry Esmond* and *The Newcomes*. The greatest writer of the age, Dickens, was at his peak: *Dombey and Son, David Copperfield, Bleak House, Hard Times, Little Dorrit, A Tale of Two Cities, Great Expectations* and *Our Mutual Friend* were all published between 1848 and 1865. By 1870 George Eliot had published *Adam Bede, The Mill on the Floss, Silas Marner, Romola* and *Felix Holt*, and was working on *Middlemarch*. Trollope had written *The Last Chronicle of Barset* and had begun the Palliser novels. If ever there was a golden age of the English novel, then this was it.

Even if Disraeli had been writing during this period, it seems unlikely that he could have really produced anything to compare with such a formidable list. What is surprising, however, is Disraeli's failure to be even interested in what was happening around him in the literary world. During the early part of his life it was notable that he read very little contemporary literature, with the exception of those works by his friend, and later colleague, Bulwer. The years between 1820 and 1840 can boast of few great novels, and Disraeli's ignorance of literary trends is perhaps not that surprising. His apparent failure, however, to read any of the major works of the leading novelists after 1840 is extremely odd, almost perverse, even in a man with so many other preoccupations. Gladstone put off a theatre visit to read Wilkie Collins's *The Woman in White*; busy statesmen could always find the time to read novels if they so wished. Disraeli's problem did not seem to be a lack of time, but of inclination; as he said to Lady Londonderry in 1857,

> I wish, like you, I could console myself with reading novels, or even writing them; but I have lost all zest for fiction, and have for many years. I have never read anything of Dickens except an extract in a newspaper, and therefore I cannot help to decide on the merits of *Little Dorrit*.[2]

As with so much he wrote, this explicit-sounding remark seems an insufficient and oversimplified response. A similar disingenuousness undermines his comment to Lady Bradford in 1879 in which he claimed not to be able to do two things at the same time, 'at least 2 who required the creative power. When I was made leader of the opposition, I was obliged to leave off writing.'[3] In the light of the rest of Disraeli's life it seems a self-effacing remark; he had been writing some of *Endymion* only the year before while he was Prime Minister. His famous comment, which was occasioned by the publication of *Daniel Deronda*, that 'When I want to read a novel, I write one', is also surely no more than a characteristic and rhetorical way of disguising an attitude towards fiction in general which we may never fully understand.

Whatever Disraeli's attitude may have been, 1870 was to be a memorable year in the world of literature. On 9 June Dickens died. Thomas Longman wrote to Disraeli the following day:

> Alas poor Dickens!! At the Club yesterday Col. Hamley told me of his merry laugh when lately he met you and him at the American Embassy and wished he 'were' (forgive me) at your end of the table, and at that moment, unknown to us, there was no Dickens!

It was just over a month before, on 2 May, that *Lothair* was launched in a flurry of excitement which caught up, not only the literary world, but most of the reading public of Britain, Europe and the United States.

The demand for the new novel was humorously described in a letter from the publisher Thomas Longman to Disraeli on 6 May:

> There has been a run upon your bankers in Paternoster Row [Longman's premises], and our last thousand is nearly gone! We shall have another thousand in hand on Wednesday next. This will be the *sixth* thousand, and I do not feel quite certain we shall not be broken before

Wednesday! I am not sure that it would not do good, now that we have nearly 5,000 in circulation. On Monday morning Mr. Mudie's house was, I am told, in a state of siege. At an early hour his supply was sent in two carts. But real subscribers and representative footmen, in large numbers were there before them.

As explained in the first chapter, the milling crowds and the bubbling curiosity were to be expected. The secrecy in which the novel had been written had given rise to a number of rumours concerning both the book's financial expectations and, of course, its content. On the first point, the *Publishers' Circular* of 16 April had said:

Mr. Disraeli's new novel, Lothair, will be published on the 2nd of May. 'The event,' says the *Athenaeum*, 'has excited considerable interest. It is reported that a proposal was made to the author of £10,000, and another of £4,000 for its use in a periodical.' It is now, however, boldly asserted that Messrs. Longman have given the right honourable author £10,000 for the copyright of his three volumes. When authorship yields such rich results, it will, as Thackeray predicted, become absolutely a respectable and respected profession, even in Philistine England.

Once publication day had passed, *The Times* of 14 May could view the matter in a more sober light:

As many as seven thousand copies are said to have already been sold of 'Lothair'. All the stories about the price given for the copyright are devoid of foundation. The London correspondent of the 'Manchester Guardian' says: − 'Mr. Disraeli unexpectedly called on Mr. Longman one day; and desired to leave the business arrangements unreservedly in his hands. Mr. Longman is said to have replied that he felt the proposal to be a high compliment, and that he would at once accept it.'

The fact that Thomas Longman had indeed the 'business arrangements unreservedly in his hands' is corroborated by a letter he wrote to Disraeli on 10 May:

Having your licence to deal with your property in 'Lothair' as if my own, I have to day accepted a cheque for *£100* for leave to print 'Lothair' in a Melbourne Newspaper called the 'Australian'. This I believe will rather help the demand there when we produce a cheaper edition, probably price six shillings, with your approval always.

Apart from the business arrangements for the book, the secrecy surrounding the matter, combined with Disraeli's desire for confidential encouragement, meant that Thomas Longman was also privy to the genesis of the novel, and the author several times asked the publisher to express any opinion or criticism he might have of the work. Longman's 'criticisms' were, in the main, eulogies, although he was able to point out the odd *faux pas*; he can claim, for example, the responsibility for having suggested that the beautiful Euphrosyne's 'almond shaped nose' be amended to the more appropriate 'almond shaped nostrils'. By 28 March Longman had finished his first reading of the novel, and he accordingly wrote to Disraeli:

> permit me to say that the grace and refinement of the concluding chapters has much struck me. The atmosphere of cultivated mind and manner pervades the whole story, and is as delightful, and refreshing, as the air of those charming old gardens full of roses, wall flowers, and sweet peas, that you describe, and not the less because all perfectly natural, though nature appears in her most graceful mode. Your story is well worthy of your motto,[4] and besides this entertainment I am sure that every lady in the land will be the better for reading it.

It was not, of course, a novel aimed solely at ladies. For all its 'grace and refinement', it was notably a novel marked by topicality. For the modern reader that topicality is no more apparent than in Disraeli's inclusion of the question of Italian nationalism. However, it seems more than likely that this side of the novel grew as an extension, both geographical and moral, of the immediate dilemma which Disraeli first envisaged for his 'hero', Lothair. Just before Christmas 1868 the young 3rd Marquess of Bute left the Church of England and became a Roman Catholic. The *Globe* of 16 April 1872 later described him as 'heir to one of the most splendid properties which it has ever fallen to the lot of a British nobleman to possess'. Disraeli based the figure of Lothair on a similar financial and aristocratic foundation; his hero has little else in common with the Marquess of Bute.

The novel's main success is the structured build-up, from its opening, to Lothair's coming of age. It is this event which will endow the hero with independence and fortune and sanction him as a legitimate prey for the adult world of conflicting factions and opinions. In his minority he had been the ward of two guardians, one of whom is a member of the Scottish Kirk and the other a new cardinal who has only recently deserted the Anglican Church for Rome, and their opposition and differing views regarding Lothair's upbringing prefigure later psychological, religious and political battles in the work. As Lothair makes his journey through the novel he appears as a quarry stalked by the Church of England, the Roman Church and the secret revolutionary societies of Europe, all of whom, while openly coveting his 'soul', have their eyes on his great wealth, position and future influence. Lothair's entanglement with all the conflicting groups involves him in intrigue, war, melodrama and escapes, and, as is often the case with a Disraelian hero, he completes his 'adventure' by touring through a good deal of Europe and the Near East. The great difference in this novel, however, is that the subject matter, far from being a pure extension of romantic psychology as it was in *Contarini Fleming*, is rather a reflection of the great struggles which were taking place in Europe (and particularly in Rome) at the time. The combination of historical as well as personal relevance is perhaps not enough to guarantee merit to a work of art. But with *Lothair* Disraeli showed a control over his subject matter which is not apparent in any other of his novels. That control does not preclude the usual Disraelian wit and extravagance, but it is a strong contributor to the argument that *Lothair* is his best novel.

When dealing with the matters of Roman Catholicism and Italian nationalism, Disraeli seems to have been content to indulge his imagination and intuition as much as his 'political' assessment of the problems. While this is another example of the way he was able to expand through fiction with a freedom which would have perhaps been impolitic in his parliamentary life, it is also an indication of the large part imagination and intuition played in his political doctrine, such as it was, in the later years of his life. His ever-present obsession with manipulating events and ordering experience and dividing issues into clearly defined dichotomies is perhaps a strong reason for criticising his political as well as his novelistic achievements. Certainly, in strictly literary terms, it is an approach which betrays a certain naivety which, compared with the major novelists of the day, undermined Disraeli's fictional products. But the world built on oppositions of Rich and Poor, Old and New Generations, or Secret Societies and Roman Catholics, was fundamentally a romantic world. While a polarisation of values could sanction an indulgence in paradox or contradiction, the oppositions involved presented the ideal setting for the 'adventure' of the romantic hero. On 21 July 1863 Disraeli wrote to his friend Mrs Brydges Willyams: 'At present the peace of the world has been preserved, not by statesmen but by capitalists ... For the last three months it has been a struggle between the secret societies and the European millionaires. Rothschild hitherto has won ... '⁵ Again the polarisation, and this time an implied, at least, distrust of the 'secret societies' – the movements for nationalism.

With his last major book before *Lothair*, that is, *Lord George Bentinck* published in 1851, Disraeli had written of the importance of these movements only three years after the European upheavals of 1848. These societies were modelled on the Lodges of eighteenth-century Freemasonry, and on the societies which had later been formed in Italy and Germany to resist the rule of Napoleon. By the mid-nineteenth century they were a widespread phenomenon in Europe, especially in forms like the 'Young Italy' and 'Young Europe' movements founded by Mazzini. The similarity of title with Young England may encourage the notion that Disraeli was in favour of such nationalistic tendencies. However, in the 1840s he was at least suspicious, if not openly distrustful, of them; Fakredeen's apparently irresponsible idea for 'Young Syria' in *Tancred*, which was written one year before the European revolutions of 1848, is a more parallel case. Certainly, once Disraeli had experience of high office his prejudices were reinforced by his acquaintance with the activities of the Fenian societies in Ireland. Prejudice rarely functions in a successful politician without some degree of expediency, and it must be said that during the 1860s Disraeli was hopeful of wooing the Catholic vote in England. It was therefore not solely his view of European nationalism as a menace to civilisation that made him decline to meet Garibaldi in London in 1864.

Not that Disraeli was in any sense blind to the capabilities of the Roman Church as an alternative political power. While *Lord George Bentinck* commented on the secret societies, it also left behind the romantic and sentimental view of the Catholic faith which had been a feature of his novels up to and including *Sybil* in 1845. Although Disraeli's mind had been moving in this direction anyway, the tone of *Lothair* on religion as well as secret societies was again determined to a great extent by his experience in office. While the activities of the Fenian societies reinforced any prejudice he may have had against underground nationalist movements, the outrages executed by the group succeeded in bringing to a head the grievances of Ireland. In the late 1860s the British government had still not realised that the root of the problem lay with land tenure, and both Liberals and Conservatives treated the issue as a mainly religious one. As part of a plan to strengthen and support both the Catholic and Presbyterian institutions in Ireland, so that they might be levelled up to something approaching the Anglican position, the Conservatives sought to grant a charter and a financial endowment for a Roman Catholic university in Dublin.

Disraeli wooed the new Archbishop of Westminster, Cardinal Manning, in the hope that he would be able to influence the Irish lobbies and hierarchy. On 10 March 1868 a private member's motion on the state of Ireland presented an opportunity for the suggestion of the plan for the new university. However, six days later Gladstone cut the ground from under Disraeli's feet on the Catholic question by announcing his view that the Anglican Establishment in Ireland should be swept away altogether. The relationship between Disraeli and Manning ended immediately. Although the plan was wrecked mainly by Gladstone's opportune sense of timing, Disraeli insisted on regarding Manning's earlier protestations of support as disingenuous. If his outlet of revenge was to be denied him in the House of Commons, he did at least have his fiction as an agent of retribution.

The novel was to refine Disraeli's prejudices into an elegant story rather than a crude piece of propaganda; but it was nevertheless a subtle re-interpretation of the influences which the author had felt from the secret societies and from the Roman Church through his life as a leading politician.

In *Lothair* the Italian nationalist movement is represented through the beautiful Theodora who, by her personal charms rather than anything else, wins Lothair to her cause for a while. He fights alongside her in what is a sketchy version of Garibaldi's abortive campaign of 1867, until she is killed at Viterbo. The episode is an important part of the plot and Lothair's 'education', but despite its part in the explicit and implicit dichotomy of the secret societies and Roman Catholicism, it is the less obviously glamorous influence of organised religion which pervades most of the novel. This tone becomes increasingly clear as it includes within itself the question of personal faith and personal destiny which was always so important to Disraeli. Despite Theodora's claim to be very religious, her 'natural' religion is not developed, nor is it seen to have any logical consequence within the terms of the novel other than military action. When Lothair tries to reason with himself, and with Cardinal Grandison (based on Manning), on what faith is, we find an echo of a dilemma which affects most of Disraeli's heroes in some way. Tancred, for example, asks 'What is DUTY, and what is FAITH? What ought I to DO, and what ought I to BELIEVE?' Grandison's answer to Lothair is clear:

'It exists in the Church,' replied the Cardinal with decision. 'All without that pale is practical atheism.'

'It seems to me that a sense of duty is natural to man,' said Lothair, 'and that there can be no satisfaction in life without attempting to fulfil it.'

'Noble words, my dear young friend; noble and true. And the highest duty of man, especially in this age, is to vindicate the principles of religion, without which the world must soon become a scene of universal desolation.' (*Lothair*, ch. xvii)

Grandison's words are purposely couched in generalities of 'the Church', rather than in any sectarian argument, and he is seen here to be giving subtle expression to the matters which are perturbing the emerging mind of his ward. Nevertheless, the overall tone of the novel leads us to seek an answer within one or another wing of the established church. As with Tancred, Lothair desires to go to the Near East to find the 'cradle' of his faith, but once again, although on one level the novel hints at a universal faith, Disraeli's own views on race and religion lead to an expression of an ordered compartmentalisation. As Paraclete the Syrian says to Lothair:

'In My Father's house are many mansions,' [John XIV, ii] and by the various families of nations the designs of the Creator are accomplished. God works by races, and one was appointed in due season and after many developments to reveal and expound in this land the spiritual nature of man. The Aryan and the Semite are of the same blood and origin, but when they quitted their central land they were ordained to follow opposite courses. Each division of the great race has developed one portion of the double nature of humanity, till after all their wanderings they met again, and, represented by their two choicest families, the Hellenes and the Hebrews, brought together the treasures of their accumulated wisdom and secured the civilisation of man. (*Lothair*, ch. lxxvii)

Although the expression is made through a 'character' the tone is too familiar for us not to recognise Disraeli's voice. It is at times like this that the original questions of faith and duty become transformed and abstracted (geographically as well, as in *Tancred*) into those theories of race and religion which are ultimately clap-trap. Once back 'home' in England, Lothair's embracing of Anglicanism bears no relation to his visit to the cradle of the church, nor does it stem from his persuasion of the doctrinal correctness of the Anglican faith. It is rather a reaction to the fact that Cardinal Grandison exceeded the limits in trying to win him over to Catholicism, and it is also an expression of a patriotism which is best aired by Lady Corisande, who represents all the wealth, beauty and status of English society:

I look upon our nobility joining the Church of Rome as the greatest calamity that has ever happened to England. Irrespective of all religious considerations, on which I will not presume to touch, it is an abnegation of patriotism; and in this age, when all things are questioned, a love of our country seems to me the one sentiment to cling to. (*Lothair*, ch. xlv)

For Disraeli 'patriotism' had a far healthier ring to it than 'nationalism', and, indeed, one would not want to stress the few absurdities of *Lothair* at the expense of his wonderfully lively but controlled picture of *English* society. Disregarding the religious questions for one moment, one of the finest things about the novel is surely its presentation of the upper levels of English society in the late 1860s. One is reminded of those comments by a critic of *Sybil* in 1845 who said: 'The exposure of the oligarchy – its heartlessness, its selfishness – is much more complete than the delineation of the lower nation; in the first case Mr. Disraeli has had the personal experience.' What we are shown in *Lothair* is a far cry from the heartlessness and selfishness of *Coningsby*'s Lord Monmouth or *Sybil*'s Lord Marney; this novel is a lucid endorsement of the aristocracy of England. And it is all the more apparent because, by 1870, it certainly *was* based on personal experience.

As far as their outward appearance is concerned, many of Disraeli's pillars of society seem banal; he was more interested in what his characters said than what they looked like. For example, of the Duke of Brecon we are told: 'His head was well-placed on his broad shoulders, and his mien was commanding.' But Disraeli more than makes up for this with his portrayal of grace, wit and manners, so that every page which shows English society sparkles with observed and heard life. The irony which was always liable to be epigrammatic, in this novel more than any of his others, clearly prefigures the style of Oscar Wilde; for example,

> St. Aldegonde held extreme opinions, especially on political affairs, being a republican of the reddest dye. He was opposed to all privilege, and indeed to all orders of men, except dukes, who were a necessity. He was also strongly in favour of the equal division of all property, except land. (*Lothair*, ch. xxi)

Every object or ornament also comes in for Disraeli's habitual praise as he indulges, yet again, his love of grandiose table decorations:

> The table seemed literally to groan under vases and gigantic flagons, and, in its midst, rose a mountain of silver, on which apparently all the cardinal virtues, several of the pagan deities, and Britannia herself, illustrated with many lights a glowing inscription. (*Lothair*, ch. viii)

It was another of the great and glittering props which always featured in his very theatrical fictional world. Against this background, however, the matter of the book was new, topical and controlled. It demonstrated Disraeli's full maturity working on what was very much the traditional pattern of his works. The 'problem' for the hero was much the same as it had always been; as Lothair says at the end of chapter xxxi, 'I perceive that life is not so simple an affair as I once supposed'. More than twenty years may have passed since the publication of his last novel, but the break in composition was not now so apparent. At one point in chapter xxx Disraeli wrote 'Tancred' in his manuscript when he meant 'Lothair'. The cynic would say that this is just another indication of how similar and characterless all Disraeli's 'heroes' were. But it is surely also a sign of the constant dream that lurks behind all Disraeli's stories.

> An American gentleman, with more than courtesy, has forwarded to me a vast number of notices of *Lothair* which have appeared in the leading journals of his country. He tells me that, irrespective of literary 'organs', there are in the Union five thousand newspapers, and it is not impossible that some notice of *Lothair* might appear in each of

> these. However various may be the opinions of those which I thus
> possess, they appear to me generally to be sincere, and in point of
> literary ability; taste, style, and critical acumen; I think they need not
> fear competition with the similar productions of our own land.

So begins the general preface which Disraeli wrote to introduce the
collected edition of his novels which was published in 1870 with
Lothair as the first volume. The preface, which is refreshingly, if typically, free of modesty, gave Disraeli the chance to review his life's work
in fiction from a position of fame and respectability. For the most part,
it is itself another extension of the ordering process within which
Disraeli interpreted his own past. It is a carefully structured review of
his literary career and it is very select in what it chooses to present. For
example, it is here that Disraeli gives his very lucid and thoughtful
account of the genesis and plan of his Young England trilogy – an
exegesis which may give little idea of the way those novels really came
fitfully into being twenty-five years before. At the same time, Disraeli
chooses to omit any reference to *The Young Duke*. While this book
was without doubt the child of prostituted circumstances, it remains
today a more readable story than some of the other early romances. Of
the other novels he wrote of *Henrietta Temple* and *Venetia*: 'These are
not political works, but they would commemorate feelings more
enduring than public passions, and they were written with care and
some delight.' The second half of *Henrietta Temple* and all of *Venetia*
were, of course, written very quickly for financial reasons; but it is true
that Disraeli was never an author to equate 'care' with the amount of
time a novel took to write. Most of his works were written in a fever of
enthusiastic passion, and there is no reason to think that he did not find
all his novels, in some way, a 'delight'.

His most important early novel, from the point of view of the reader
trying to understand the author, must surely be *Contarini Fleming*.
Contarini was also Disraeli's favourite child – a child which, perhaps,
did not fulfil its great potential, both as an earner of funds and, in
retrospect, as a work of art:

> It was almost stillborn, and having written it with deep thought and
> feeling, I was naturally discouraged from further effort. Yet the
> youthful writer who may, like me, be inclined to despair, may learn
> also from my example not to be precipitate in his resolves ... it would
> have been better if a subject so essentially psychological had been
> treated at a more mature period of life.

And what of *Vivian Grey*, that very first novel which dogged him
through the whole of his public life? It certainly did seem to have a self-
sustaining life of its own. Disraeli recognised this; there was a point
when excuses had to come to an end:

'Vivian Grey' is essentially a puerile work, but it has baffled even the efforts of its creator to suppress it. Its fate has been strange; and not the least remarkable thing is, that forty-four years after its first publication, I must ask the indulgence of the reader, for its continued and inevitable re-appearance.

Whatever it was that made Disraeli a novelist, was as alive in the 1870s as it was in 1826. Despite the many calls on his attention as Leader of the Opposition, he was sufficiently invigorated by the success of *Lothair* and the collected edition to begin a new novel. It is difficult to know if, at this stage, he ever envisaged being Prime Minister again. Certainly, he was getting no younger, and as he moved into his late sixties events began to place more of a strain on him. It was against a background of murmuring discontent that he managed to find his strength at just the right time. The great public speeches made to mass audiences at the Manchester Free Trade Hall on 3 April 1872 and at the Crystal Palace on the following 24 June, although perhaps not now regarded as the statement of radical Toryism they were once seen to be, still represented for Disraeli a *personal* stamp of authority over his party. It was as well that his position as leader was consolidated when it was, for Disraeli was soon to face a great personal loss.

On 15 December 1872 his wife Mary Anne died. It was a great blow to him. She was twelve years older than her husband and in her eightieth year, but, despite the fact that she had been ill for some time, her constant ability to share his enthusiasm, coupled with his own occasional infirmity, had always made the age difference less apparent. She was buried outside the east end of Hughenden Church on a bitterly cold winter day, with the rain pouring down. As he stood by the open grave, mourning the loss of his companion for more than thirty years of parliamentary life, it must have been hard for Disraeli to have foreseen then the spectacular nature of the years that lay ahead. Little over a year later Parliament was dissolved; *The Times* of 23 January 1874, while announcing the dissolution, also contained three columns of Gladstone's election address. In the ensuing election Disraeli and the Conservatives won a memorable victory and a strong majority in the House of Commons. For the first time in his life Disraeli had a position of real power.

It is not necessary here to discuss the political achievements and failures of Disraeli's six years in power. Yet it would be misleading not to see his last literary work against the background of his often spectacularly eventful premiership. As far as domestic legislation was concerned, the most fruitful session was that of 1875 – a session made notably smoother for Disraeli by Gladstone's formal retirement. It was this year which produced much of the social reform which has always been linked with this administration: two Trade Union Acts; the Public

Health Act; the Artisans Dwelling Act, aimed at clearing slums; the Agricultural Holdings Act, intended to alleviate tenants' grievances; another Factory Act, which sought to lessen exploitation; and the Sale of Food and Drugs Act.

There is no doubt, however, that Disraeli's leadership between 1874 and 1880 will be remembered most vividly as a period marked by foreign events and Britain's participation in them. After some years of Liberal domination, it was Disraeli's administration which put the stamp of empire on the 1870s. There was the Royal Titles Bill of 1876 by which Queen Victoria sought to become Empress of India. The previous autumn Disraeli had made his famous purchase of the Khedive's interest in the Suez Canal Company. As with so many other things, Disraeli interpreted, or chose to present, this notable event in a way which was at least an elaboration of, it not a sheer disregard for, the 'facts'. He wrote to Lady Bradford on 24 November:

> We have had all the gamblers, capitalists, financiers of the world organized and platooned in bands of plunderers, arrayed against us, and secret emissaries in every corner, and have baffled them all, and have never been suspected. The day before yesterday, Lesseps, whose company has the remaining shares, backed by the French whose agent he was, made a great offer. Had it succeeded, the whole of the Suez Canal would have belonged to France and they might have shut it up.[6]

This was poppycock; the purchase was a considerable coup for Disraeli, but failure to have achieved it would not have signalled disaster for Britain, or meant a loss of control over imperial India.

A matter of more urgency was the Eastern Question, which had loomed large again earlier that year for the first time since the Crimean War. It was a problem which was vividly brought home to thousands of Britons when the *Daily News* of 23 June 1876 published an account of the atrocities by Turkish troops against Bulgarian peasants. Although Disraeli seriously misjudged public feeling over these atrocities, he was to have a chance to play the statesman in a successful light two years later at the Congress of Berlin. As with several of the events of this period of Disraeli's life, history has been romanticised through the many anecdotes and myths which have surrounded accounts of the enterprise. There is no doubt that the odd Englishman, by his very appearance and manner, encouraged such an interpretation, and, in the midst of European friction, the fashionable worlds of London and Berlin enjoyed the air of mystery which Disraeli carried with him. Amongst the society entourages which arrived at Berlin, stories of his glamorous youth were rife, and his novels, *Henrietta Temple* in particular, were read with renewed interest. Bismarck was later to remark of him: 'I must say that in spite of his fantastic novel-writing he is a capable statesman.'[7]

Capable he certainly was, but he was not by now physically strong. In 1876 he had left the House of Commons to lead the government from the upper chamber as the Earl of Beaconsfield, and if the high point of his diplomatic career was his role at the Congress of Berlin, then it should not be forgotten how much of the detailed work there was done by Lord Salisbury. After Berlin things did not go well. Although Disraeli can escape much of the blame on a personal level, events in Afghanistan and the Zulu War were undoubtedly symptomatic of his failure to oversee vigorously certain important foreign affairs. Disraeli's imagination and deftness had helped him to steer a course through several difficult foreign problems, but in the end his electoral defeat was brought about largely by his apparent failure to control events. He was at his best when he was creating and manipulating affairs but, increasingly, as his health failed, he was found to be rather waiting on events. During the crisis over the Eastern Question, when Disraeli was trying to balance the Turkish interest against the Russian one, a lady of fashion called across to him at a banquet: 'What are you waiting for, Lord Beaconsfield?' Unruffled, he replied, 'At this moment for the potatoes, madam.'[8] If the old skill in repartee, fiction and politics remained with him to the end, the increasing bouts of inactivity were a sign that much of the former vigour had departed.

In chapter xliv of *Endymion* Myra, the sister of the hero, says to Lord Roehampton: 'I cannot imagine a position more unfortunate than that of an exiled prince.' 'I can,' says Lord Roehampton in reply. 'To have the feelings of youth and the frame of age.' When Disraeli revealed to his secretary, Montagu Corry, in 1878, that he had been writing another novel, he also made some comments on the task of an author:

> 'The greatest stretch of intellect in the world is to write a first rate work of fiction. It requires first rate "narrative power", first rate description and first rate dramatic power and above [all] a sense of humor.'
> As a general rule Lord B. would lay it down to be more difficult to be a great writer of fiction than a great speaker. Certainly his experience is that a great effort to be the former is the most exhausting.[9]

When Disraeli finished *Endymion* he was 75 years old. He had been aged further than his years by being Prime Minister. He maintained right to the end of his life the characteristic humour and vivacity which were to be found in all his writings and conversations. But, in many ways, *Endymion* is a tired book, and it lacks that vital spark of originality. Rather than being another adventure in its own right, it is a remembrance and a restatement of past adventures, dreams and ideas. Disraeli probably began writing the novel in 1870, encouraged by the success of *Lothair*. By the time he became Prime Minister, over half the book had been written, and chapters lxi–lxxviii were probably written in 1878 while he was in office. The final chapters were completed in May, June and July 1880, after his defeat in the general election in April.[10] It was only in August of that year that Disraeli asked Corry to read the manuscript:

> Read it at once my dear fellow for the purpose of seeing if the story and the work in general be fit to publish. If you condemn it I will burn it. And then I would ask you to read it a second time to see if it be in English; and then again a third time to review the spelling and punctuation.[11]

Needless to say, Corry did not condemn it.

It was he who was responsible for the ensuing negotiations with Thomas Norton Longman, the son of the Thomas Longman who had published *Lothair*. The detailed story of the publication of *Endymion* has been well told by Annabel Jones,[12] but there are two particular points which must be repeated here. First, it was extremely unusual that the negotiations for the sale of the book, which began in July 1880, took place when neither Corry nor Longman had read the manuscript. Even with a very eminent author like George Eliot, John Blackwood had refused to accept *Felix Holt* without having first seen it; it was not that he doubted her talent, but that 'it would be against the principle upon which I really enter into and take a pleasure in my own business were I to decide finally on such a matter without having some opportunity of forming an opinion of the book by seeing a volume or so'.[13]

The second unusual point was the sum of money paid to the author. George Eliot had been offered £10,000 for *Romola* (1863) by Smith, Elder, for the entire copyright, but she turned it down in favour of an offer by which the copyright reverted to her after six years. Dickens over a period of twenty months between 1846 and 1848 had earned £9,000 from *Dombey and Son*. Novel-writing could now be very lucrative, and by the time he wrote his autobiography Trollope had earned £70,000 from his works. Nevertheless, the sum of £10,000 which Longman paid Disraeli for the copyright of *Endymion* in 1880 was the largest single amount ever paid for a work of fiction in the nineteenth century. Disraeli wrote to Lady Bradford to say that he accepted the amount 'with a scruple, such a sum never having before been given for a work of fiction, or indeed any other work',[14] but it seems he decided to sell the copyright, instead of taking a royalty agreement, knowing that he would soon die. During 1878, when he felt he might not live to finish it, Disraeli, in what can only be seen as another spasm of eccentricity, left Corry a note telling him how the story was supposed to end, so that the secretary would be able to finish it and publish it post-humously. As it was, the lump sum received for the work had the practical significance of allowing Disraeli, who had been without a London home since the death of his wife, to secure a seven-year lease on 19 Curzon Street in January 1881.

By September 1880 the manuscript was ready to be collected and Longman travelled to Hughenden to receive it and to pay his cheque to Disraeli. The manuscript was immediately set on his return to London, and the proofs had all been read by 7 October. During the middle of that month Disraeli suffered a severe attack of gout which incapacitated him for several weeks, and on 12 November he travelled to London to see his doctor. While there he had one meeting with Longman before returning to Hughenden on 18 November. Just over a week later, on 26 November, *Endymion* was published, only ten weeks after Thomas Longman took possession of the manuscript.

The book sold well, but not so well as to immediately justify the £10,000 which Longman paid for it. Disraeli's conscience was again to the fore, and there is the hint that the author realised that the book in no way compared with *Lothair*. By March 1881 he was writing to the publisher offering to cancel the former arrangement in favour of a royalty agreement. Longman, however, refused to accept the offer. The first edition had admittedly not sold as well as expected, but a cheap edition issued early in 1881 boosted the turnover. Finally Corry was able to note:

> Mr. Longman visited me at 19 Curzon St., a few days before Lord Beaconsfield's death, and authorized me to inform Lord B:— who heard the intelligence with extreme satisfaction – that his firm had just turned the corner and was beginning to make a profit out of the bargain.
>
> I believe that this was the last piece of business on wh: he and I spoke together.
>
> After so many! and such![15]

The critics and Disraeli's friends were kinder in their comments about this book than they had been about *Lothair*. Disraeli was now a respected elder statesman near to death, and one suspects that the kindness of the reception was not all due to the merits of the novel; the subject matter is dealt with fondly rather than passionately or wittily.

The story begins at the time of Disraeli's youth, in 1827. From Canning's death it moves leisurely through the next thirty years of political life, to end with the defeat of the Coalition government in 1855. It therefore covers with its own bizarre and unlikely romance those years which saw the author of *Vivian Grey* rise to become Chancellor of the Exchequer. Drawing on such a large time-span, the novel also displays, in an extreme way, the author's tendency to base his characters on real figures in public life. The criticism which Monckton Milnes made in 1847 to this effect is nowhere more applicable than with regard to *Endymion*. There is Palmerston (Lord Roehampton), Louis Napoleon (Florestan), the Rothschilds (the Neuchatels), George Smythe (Waldershare), Bismarck (Count Ferrol), Metternich (Baron Sergius), Cobden (Thornberry) and many more. Even Thackeray appears in a rather snide caricature (he had, after all, died seventeen years before) as St Barbe. Endymion himself, Disraeli claimed, was based on Sir Charles Dilke, although there would seem to be no similarity. Dilke took the comparison as a compliment, presumably as Endymion rises to be Prime Minister. However, the 'hero' is a faint and vapid creature who evolves through the novel merely from a 12-year-old innocent and idealistic boy to a 40-year-old innocent and idealistic man.

Archbishop Tait finished the novel 'with a painful feeling that the writer considers all political life as mere play and gambling',[16] but for all the book's 'political' background, it is not really about politics. Once again, Disraeli's fiction shows itself not to be about partisan issues, but rather about principled conduct and the acquisition of power. It is another romantic rise to fame and prestige as Endymion, who begins his career as a clerk, climbs to the top of the greasy pole. In this sense the tale is very familiar, and as we read this last complete work by Disraeli, every facet of it seems to reinforce that familiarity.

Endymion is 'withdrawn from his school and deprived of his university', as Disraeli felt he had been; but the hero finds in the companionship of Waldershare 'a rich compensation'. Where Vivian Grey had scorned university life in favour of the 'world', Endymion finds under the roof of Mr Bertie Tremaine (probably Bulwer) 'a large body of young men of breeding, of high education, and full of ambition, that was a substitute for the society, becoming his youth and station, which he had lost by not going to the university'. When we read of the dishes of ortolans and the 'dazzling tiaras and flashing rivières' on the fashionable ladies of Endymion's society, we are reminded of how Disraeli's fascination with the ornaments of affluence had always accompanied *his* rise through society. Through the exuberance of Waldershare Disraeli lives again the ideals and dreams of Young England; while through the character's faults the author can fondly admit the ephemeral nature of such dreams: '"He is a wonderful man – Mr. Waldershare," said Mr. Vigo to Rodney, "but I fear not practical."' The questions of *Coningsby* and *Sybil* rise again, if only as items in a conversation, and the problems of political allegiance, the condition of England and the Chartists drift across the page. Baron Sergius's remarks, meanwhile, send us back to *Tancred* and *Lord George Bentinck*:

No man will treat with indifference the principles of race. It is the key of history, and why history is often so confused is that it has been written by men who were ignorant of this principle and all the knowledge it involves. (*Endymion*, ch. lvi)

Mr Sidney Wilton's remark that 'You have no conception of the devices and resources of the secret societies of Europe' reminds us of the prejudices which helped to shape *Lothair*, while Nigel Penruddock (a kinder portrayal of Cardinal Manning) breathes a form of religion which, unlike that in *Lothair*, looks back to the vision of faith, chivalry and history that we found in *Sybil*.

However, if much of *Endymion* contributes to a delightful and animated glance back at the days and thoughts which formed the young novelist Disraeli, there are also signs that the familiarity is partly due to a waning imagination or tiredness. The reappearance of the name of Mr Tadpole briefly may give some hint at continuity of purpose, but too often the names of people suggest that Disraeli's pool of characters is running dry. Why call the most famous mantua-maker in London Madame Euphrosyne, when the name has been used of a more major character in *Lothair*? Could not Disraeli have thought of a name for St Barbe's publishers other than 'Shuffle and Screw', the name of the 'bad' factory owners in *Sybil*? Similarly, many of the phrases seem steeped in the memories of the past. Even seemingly insignificant words contribute to the slight sense of delirium one has when reading the novel. The worker Enoch's term '*inveterate* capitalist' is exactly the same as the worker Field's in *Sybil*; where Contarini Fleming's success at school was encapsulated in the phrase 'In a word, I was popular', we are told of the hero of Disraeli's last book 'In a word Endymion was popular'. They may seem small points, but the cumulative effect of such a style is one of languor. When the novel was published many people picked it up with the hope that it would be autobiographical. This element was, however, found to be practically non-existent in the novel; the book was a 'romance', and the *Standard* informed would-be readers that if they looked for autobiography in its pages they would be disappointed. The familiarity of the pages was not one inspired by candid memory, but rather by an obsessive ideal. Like most of Disraeli's fiction, it was not the history of a life, but the history of a dream of a life.

Disraeli died at half past four on the morning of Tuesday 19 April 1881. His love of fiction had not ended with *Endymion*, for he left behind him nine chapters and the beginning of a tenth of a new untitled novel.[17] This fragment has been called *Falconet*, after its main character, and it shows a directness and topicality which may or may not have been a conscious reaction to the faults of *Endymion*. It is intriguing to think that Disraeli's strengths as a novelist were finally awakened, not by the dream of his own life, but by the reality of his arch rival, 'that unprincipled maniac', Gladstone. It would appear that *Falconet* was intended as a satire on the man who had now returned to lead the Liberals again as Prime Minister. Yet if it was Gladstone that inspired this last effort of creation, it must be remarked that the fragment does not show signs of having been composed in anger or hatred. It says a good deal for Disraeli's talent as a novelist that his artistic integrity often had a healthy independence of his political views. Yet, paradoxically, it is also true that much of his writing was political, in that it was so often unashamedly manipulative in the way it interpreted life, and in the way it sought to make the reader see life.

Notes: Chapter 8

1 Gordon S. Haight (ed.), *The George Eliot Letters* (London: Oxford University Press; New Haven, Conn.: Yale University Press, 1954), Vol. I, pp. 192–3.
2 Quoted by E. A. Horsman, *On the Side of the Angels?* (Dunedin: University of Otago Press, n.d.), p. 46.
3 Quoted by Vernon Bogdanor in his introduction to *Lothair* (London: Oxford University Press, 1975), p. vii.
4 'Nosse omnia haec salus est adolescentulis' (Terentius: 'All this is salvation to a young man.')
5 Quoted by Robert Blake, *Disraeli* (London: Eyre & Spottiswoode, 1966), p. 430.
6 Quoted in ibid., pp. 584–5.
7 Quoted in ibid., p. 679.
8 Quoted in ibid., p. 653.
9 Quoted in ibid., pp. 732–3.
10 Robert Blake, 'The dating of *Endymion*', *Review of English Studies*, n.s., vol. 17, no. 66 (1966).
11 Quoted by Blake, *Disraeli*, p. 734.
12 Annabel Jones, 'Disraeli's *Endymion*: a case study', in *Essays in the History of Publishing*, ed. Asa Briggs (London: Longman, 1974).
13 Quoted in ibid., p. 153.
14 Quoted in ibid., p. 153.
15 Quoted by Blake, *Disraeli*, p. 735.
16 Quoted in ibid., p. 735.
17 Printed as an appendix to Vol. V of W. F. Monypenny and G. E. Buckle, *The Life of Benjamin Disraeli, Earl of Beaconsfield*, 6 vols (London: John Murray, 1910–20).

Index

DATE DUE			

Braun   181835